CLEMSON™
THROUGH THE EYES
OF THE TIGER

DAVID -

A true Friend

AND PATRIOT.

Go Tigers!!

John Selketa

by the Clemson™ Mascots and Friends

Semper Fi!!

First Edition
ISBN 978-4951-7541-1

Printed by PIP in Anderson, South Carolina

For more information about this book, contact
john106publishing@gmail.com

John106Publishing
106 Ridgeview Drive
Clemson, SC 29631

CLEMSON™ THROUGH THE EYES OF THE TIGER

by the Clemson™ Mascots and Friends

Editors
Karen Blackman, Sam Blackman, Tim Bourret, Miriam Coffman, Danny Gregg, Kathy Hunter, and Kathryn Smith

Graphics
Sam Blackman, Megan Fallow, Justin Green, Jeff Kallin, Kat Lawhon, Phillip Sikes, Tiger Town Graphics, and Brandon Wilson

Photographers
Kelly Adams, Frank Alexander, Atlanta 2 News, Bart Boatwright, Mark Crammer, Carolina Panthers, Chrystelle Ensley, Clemson University Athletics, Clemson University Special Collections, Eddie Cliffe, Jason Ray Foundation, Wilton E. Hall, A. Hodges, Jim Graham, Kenneth Jordan, Greenville Road Warriors, *Greenville News*, Jeff Herbert, Margaret Le, Dawson Powers, Miami Dolphins, Myrtle Beach Pelicans, Pi Kappa Alpha, Randy Rampey, Glen Spake, Bob Waldrop, and Patrick Wright

Dedicated to all the amateur and professional photographers at sporting events who capture that special moment. To the announcers and writers who report what everyone witnessed for those not in attendance. To all the student-athletes, cheerleaders, dancers, bands, and mascots for sacrificing their time to make "Something Special in These Hills." Finally, to all those young and old who have traveled from around the world to visit this unique college town community in South Carolina. Thank you! Together, you have made Clemson "In Season Every Season."

CONTENTS

FOREWORD

Some of the lyrics of the Bob Seger song "Turn the Page" could be written about the life of a mascot: "You feel the eyes upon you...Most times you can't hear 'em talk...Every ounce of energy you try to give away...There I am, up on the stage..."

As you turn the pages of this book, you will read stories about some of the experiences of the students who have portrayed the Clemson University mascots, The Tiger and the Tiger Cub*. We hope they will become a history lesson for all who love Clemson, and that they will last forever as readers pass them along at a family gathering, a tailgate, on a sports talk show or with a weekly lunch group.

The question remains the same and the answer never changes: "Is it hot in there?" Anyone who played the role of the Clemson Tiger or Tiger Cub has been asked this question over and over.

Every Clemson fan has probably had a picture or interaction with one of the mascots over the past 65 years.

It could have been me who held your baby on a 95-degree day while you tried to snap a picture. Of course, I couldn't tell you that the lens cover was still on your camera due to our mascot code, the "No Talk Rule." I often wonder why you felt so comfortable giving your newborn to a sweating college student.

Pictures are easy. However, signing autographs is very difficult for us with only three fingers and a thumb surrounded by fur. We have no grip and are not able to pull the cap off your pen. Once again, the "No Talk Rule" had me gesturing for assistance.

You allowed us to reach into that tub of popcorn and literally throw it in our faces as if we were eating it. Then we put our arms around your girlfriend or spouse for a picture, and you think it's great when we start flirting with them. Finally, as your child misbehaved by grabbing our tail, we placed them in the trash can, and you laughed while taking another picture.

Why do you let us do this? Because The Tiger and Tiger Cub are playful, trustworthy characters who value your prized possessions as one of their own.

We don't grow up with the ambition of being a mascot. "There's Something in These Hills" which enabled us to find our destiny to become either The Tiger or the Tiger Cub. Everyone has their own stories.

I recall being introduced to Clemson in 1990 by way of my sister Allison. She had chosen to attend Clemson, a university 720 miles away from our home in Pennsylvania. Our family made the trip to Clemson three times a year to see her march in Tiger Band and watch the Tigers play.

I was the class clown of my high school so I was somewhat prepared for being a college mascot. Three years later, after enrolling in Clemson, while moving equipment for Tiger Band, I was fortunate enough to meet Chase Nichols, who was the current Tiger. Chase was the person who encouraged me to attend tryouts with the goal of becoming the next Tiger.

A small fraction of the former and current Clemson students have had the opportunity to be one of our mascots, goodwill ambassadors for

our university. To be the most popular person (creature) on campus, it was just like being Superman, even though you didn't know who we really were outside of the suit.

Today, I am still The Tiger and like my counterparts, will always be The Tiger. Since 1998, I have been judging our mascot tryouts, which allows me a chance to know each new Tiger. We all have been introduced to someone as the Clemson Tiger.

In 2014, I made it my mission to reach out to every Tiger and Tiger Cub mascot for a reunion. Some of us had never met, but that didn't matter. Our names are listed on the back of the push-up board and I always wondered who these people were. When it all came together, the day was magical as I saw a bunch of "me's" dating back to the '50s. There was not enough time to tell all the stories as we lined up on the field that Homecoming evening to be welcomed back to Clemson. We had the opportunity to be honored outside of the suit, together as one. Of all of my memories at Clemson, this was the greatest!

What you are about to read are some stories that have been kept secret for years. I hope you enjoy our insight into a great experience, "Clemson through the Eyes of The Tiger."

Oh yeah...it was and still is hot in the suit.

–Mike Bays, The Tiger 1994-97

* Some of the mascots in the '50s and '60s were omitted due to the lack of accurate information from one or more source. If you were one of these mascots, please contact the author or one of the mascots listed so your story can be added to future publications of this book. Thank you.

** A portion of the proceeds from the sale of this book will be given to a fund for the mascots to make annual appearances at area children hospitals. If you would like to contribute to this fund, please call the IPTAY Office at 864-656-2115.

CHAPTER ONE
THE 1950s

ROY SOUTHERLIN
No. 1 Tiger Early 1950s
Bachelor of Science in Textile Manufacturing '54
Retired
Phillips Industries and Powers Pneumatic Controls
Residence - Dunnellon, Fla.
Hometown - Marietta, S.C.

It is not certain when The Tiger began appearing at Clemson athletic events; however, below is a picture of The Tiger at the January 1, 1952 Gator Bowl. It was the second of two consecutive bowl games against the University of Miami. The brown boxer dog is Hurricane I, the first official mascot for the Miami Hurricanes. He started roaming the Miami sidelines in 1950.

The Tigers won the first matchup against the Hurricanes in the 1951 Orange Bowl, 15-14. A year later, the Hurricanes returned the favor with a win at the 1952 Gator Bowl.

Final Score: Miami 14   #19 Clemson 0

From 1942 to 1967, the football team dressed and walked from the Clemson Field House (renamed Fike Field House in 1966) to Memorial Stadium. As the players approached the stadium, you could hear the clacking of their spikes on the road.

So how did I become The Tiger? I was self-appointed. I found the suit in a closet in the Clemson Field House. You can't become a superhero unless you try on a costume, so that's what I did. It was a great way to meet girls, get free meals from the training table and   other freebies. Wow, what a blast!

I teamed up with Jim Johnson from Charlotte, N.C. who dressed up as a leprechaun. We did our antics as a team chasing the mascots from the other schools.

The Clemson-Georgia Tech football series dates back to 1898 when the Tigers won the first four meetings between the two schools. In 1953, a Georgia Tech fraternity member jerked The Tiger head from my grasp and made off with the prize possession. After mustering a bevy of "good ole boys" from Clemson who were at the Atlanta Biltmore hotel, we marched to the fraternity house and retrieved the headgear in short order. We won the battle, but not the war, on this Saturday afternoon.

Final Score: Georgia Tech 20   Clemson 6

I apologize that over 60 years later I don't have the stories the current mascots can tell; however, I am proud to see that being The Tiger is a Clemson tradition.

TOMMY GRANT
No. 1 Tiger 1957-58
Bachelor of Science in Textile Manufacturing '58
Hometown - Ware Shoals, S.C.

BILL McCOWN
No. 1 Tiger 1959-60
Bachelor of Science in Forestry '60
Founding Director and Retired President
Dedicated Community Bank
Residence and Hometown-Darlington, S.C.

Like those before and after me, one member of the cheerleading squad was asked to be The Tiger. I was told, "Here's the suit, and you're in charge of it, so keep it clean." My solution was to put it in the shower and then hang it out of my barracks (now the fraternity quad) room window to air dry.

What was special about the 1959 season was that it was the last time the Tigers would have to travel to Columbia for the annual "Big Thursday" game held during State Fair Week. During the game, I interceptted an errant pass from the South Carolina quarterbck while standing on the Clemson sideline. The next thing you know, Coach Frank Howard was waving me towards the end zone as I ran by the Clemson bench.

Coach Howard's Tigers didn't need my assisance as the team carried him off the field after the game blowing a good-bye kiss to the "Big Thursday" tradition. The next day, the *Charlotte Observer* had a drawing of my interception along with a write-up about the game.

Final Score: #17 Clemson 27 South Carolina 0

New Year's Day 1959 saw the 8-2 Atlantic Coast Conference football champion Clemson Tigers in the Big Easy to play the Tigers of Louisiana State University in the Sugar Bowl. The game was played in Tulane Stadium with LSU being led by Heisman Trophy winner Billy Cannon. We lost a hard-fought battle to the nation's No. 1 team. It was Clemson's first game in school history versus the No. 1 team in the country.

Final Score: #1 LSU 7 #12 Clemson 0

The head cheerleader was Erwin Abell. Erwin, our wives and seven children are like brothers and sisters. This is Clemson and what it gives you for life: friendship.

Fifty-five years later, I got to meet many of the students who carried on the mascot tradition that began in the late 1940s and early 1950s. Mike Bays did a wonderful job of organizing this 2014 reunion. However, young man, next time pick me up at my parking spot! I'm not walking. And please have another reunion soon.

CHAPTER TWO
THE 1960s

STEVE MORRISON
No. 1 Tiger 1960-61
Bachelor of Science in Civil Engineering '63
Industrial Building Construction
Residence - Myrtle Beach, S.C.
Hometown - Hartsfield, S.C.

I followed my roommate Bill McCown who was The Tiger the previous year. During my year as The Tiger, McCown was the cannoneer (a military term to define a soldier who fires artillery in support of infantry). By the end of my senior year, I had been The Tiger, the cannoneer, and the head cheerleader.

The greatest feeling I had being The Tiger was at the historic first game against South Carolina to be played in Clemson. During that game, Bill fired the cannon towards an intoxicated South Carolina fan. The pressure from the blank shell caused the fan to lose his hat as he fell backwards. Like this fan, the Gamecocks fell to the Tigers in Memorial Stadium.

Final Score: Clemson 12   South Carolina 2

Since this first historic win in Death Valley (Memorial Stadium's nickname since 1948), the Tigers are 17-10-1 at home and 16-11 at Williams -Brice Stadium in Columbia going into the 2015 season against their in-state rival.

JIM LLOYD
No. 1 Tiger 1961-62
Bachelor of Science in Education '62
Deceased 2015

It is very sad to announce that we lost a member of the Clemson Family when Jim Lloyd passed away during the writing of this book. Mr. Lloyd was looking forward to submitting his stories about his experiences as The Tiger after a vacation with his wife Karen.

ROBERT "BOB" TROGDON
No. 1 Tiger 1962-63
Bachelor of Arts in English '63
Retired Commercial Pilot
Delta Airlines
Residence - Atlanta, Ga.
Hometown - Spartanburg, S.C.

Like most mascots during the early years, I was allowed to climb up on the crossbar of the goal post prior to the game. Then we climbed again during the game when the Tigers were headed in the opposite direction of where we were sitting. Having a high school gymnastics background definitely gave me an advantage with this antic.

Today, I look at the collapsible goal post in Death Valley and think how much easier it would be to get up on the crossbar if I stood on it as they raised it back in place before a game. Technology is great; however, rule changes have taken the fun out of the game for the current mascots.

The last two games of the 1962 season were very memorable. The first unforgettable memory was at the University of Maryland located in College Park, Md. Whenever Clemson travels to Maryland it is customary to visit the historic sites of Washington. Everyone knows college students like to sleep in, and tourist sites are not high on their list. Several of us thought it was more important to sleep than to visit the 35th President of the United States, John F. Kennedy, in the White House. A year later, when President Kennedy was assassinated, I realized that choosing to sleep was a mistake on my part.

The next day, I was walking into Byrd Stadium on the Maryland campus holding The Tiger head in my hands. All of a sudden, I was surrounded by Maryland students trying to steal the head. On this day, they never got the head because some of the Clemson football players came to my rescue.

Final Score: Clemson 17 Maryland 14

A week later South Carolina came to Tigertown for the season finale. Many families in the state of South Carolina are split, with half the family cheering for the Gamecocks and the other half for the Tigers. On this afternoon, two Spartanburg natives were on the opposite side of the field as mascots. Bobby Dowdeswell was Cocky and I was The Tiger.

With 1:42 remaining in the game, Rodney Rogers kicked the winning field goal for the Tigers. It was the second week in a row Rodney had won the game. The previous week he accomplished the feat with 1:24 remaining.

Final Score: Clemson 20 South Carolina 17

On Sunday afternoon prior to the beginning of football season, I went on a blind date with Mary Petry Stewart from Converse College. It was love at first sight. When you have met the girl of your dreams, what do you do? You invite her to all your home football games. Then as the mascot, you take off during the middle of a game through the crowd to see her sitting in the stands. After raising your headgear, you get that little kiss that helps you endure the heat of wearing the headgear throughout the remainder of the game. I am happy to say that Mary and I have been married since 1965. We have two children and five grandchildren.

After a year as The Tiger, I was the cannoneer the next year. Although you are a lot more comfortable out of the suit, you still have to worry about the opposing fans. While attending a game at Duke, members of one of their fraternities took the cannon. It was returned after they had painted it blue with a Blue Devil design on the front of the dolly, the cart with wheels on which the cannon is mounted for easy transportation.

Final Score: Duke 35 Clemson 30

JIM GIBSON
No. 1 Tiger 1963-64
Bachelors of Arts in History '65
Juris Doctor '68
University of Georgia
Retired Attorney
Howell, Gibson and Hughes Law Firm
Residence - Beaufort, S.C.
Hometown - Sumter, S.C.

I need to say thank you to Tommy Page, who was the head cheerleader. He asked, and I agreed, to become the next Tiger. The suit was a cheap costume made out of cloth. Nothing like today's suit.

Unlike the change made to the location of the Clemson-South Carolina game which is now alternated between schools, we played Georgia Tech at Historic Grant Field in Atlanta until 1974. On this day, the historic field was ankle deep in water. What a mess!

Final Score: #9 Georgia Tech 27   Clemson 0

Two weeks later it was 84 degrees in Clemson when the Georgia Bulldogs visited Death Valley. Unfortunately, there was a sudden cold snap during the first half of the game. As the temperature plunged to 57 degrees, it began to rain, and then the rain turned to golf ball-size hail which covered the field. Fans began to panic as they raced for protection under the stands. The second half was delayed for 30 minutes due to the weather conditions. Today, weather technology allows game management officials enough time to warn fans to proceed to a safe location away from lightning, heavy rain, and hail.

Final Score: Clemson 7   Georgia 7

On Friday, November 22, 1963, President Kennedy was assassinated, prompting the rescheduling of our football game against South Carolina. The next week who could forget the picture of John Kennedy, Jr. standing next to his older sister Caroline, saluting his father's casket as it was carried by a horse-drawn caisson to Arlington Cemetery? Three days later we played South Carolina. It was the only time the two rivals have battled each other on Thanksgiving Day.

Final Score: Clemson 24   South Carolina 20

Not many students had cars, so in front of the old library (now Sikes Hall) there was an area known as the "Bumming Line." One sign read "Greenville" and the other "Columbia." Thumbing a ride home was easy; returning was a different story. There was an unwritten code that if you found a ride back you would share it with fellow students.

Dr. R. C. Edwards was considered to be one of Clemson's most popular presidents, serving 1958-79. One Saturday when I was home in Sumter, Dr. Edwards called the house. He and Dean Ken Vickery (for whom Vickery Hall is named), the comptroller, would be returning to Clemson on Sunday after a meeting in Sumter. We were familiar with each other because his two-year-old granddaughter Laura Reid was always around me at the football pep rallies.

To say I was surprised was an understatement. When I hung up the phone, my father asked who had called and I said, "Dr. Edwards." My father said, "I don't need any of your smart answers." He, like two of my friends who thought it was a joke, finally believed me when Dr. Edwards picked us up the next day.

During my year as The Tiger, I was dating my future wife Louise "Wheezie" Willimon, daughter of Gene Willimon. Gene was the business manager for Clemson Athletics and the executive secretary of IPTAY. IPTAY, which stood for I Pay Ten A Year, is an organization founded in 1934 to raise money for student-athlete scholarships by having members donate $10 per year.

JERRY BURTON
The Tiger Who Wasn't a No. 1 Tiger in 1963
Bachelor of Science in Textile Management
Retired Vice President for Asset Management
Wachovia
Residence - Columbia, S.C.
Hometown - Calhoun Falls, S.C.

In 1963, I went to the movie theater in downtown Clemson to watch "Four For Texas," a movie featuring the breath-taking Ursula Andress, Dean Martin, and Frank Sinatra. (Today, the movie theatre is the Tiger Sports Shop.) My wristwatch stopped during the movie, so I missed my 4 p.m. cheerleading group picture for *TAPS*. When the yearbook came out, I was listed as being The Tiger in the picture even though I never had my picture taken.

After graduation, I was away from home serving in the U.S. Army. While away, my mom had looked through the 1964 *TAPS* and told all her family and friends that I was The Tiger.

Upon returning home, I remember one day being with some friends and my sister, Kathy. Kathy was telling them that I was The Tiger when I was in college. I told her and the group it was a mistake and how I missed the group picture. Kathy was proud of her brother and said, "Yes you were, Mom said that you were!" I guess I should have agreed because I had printed proof. It was in *TAPS*.

MARVIN "POAG" REID
No. 1 Tiger 1965-66
Bachelor of Science in
*   Pre-Professional Studies '68*
Doctor of Veterinary Medicine '71
University of Georgia
Veterinarian
Residence - Pendleton, S.C.
Hometown - Rock Hill, S.C.

In 1965, we defeated NC State (21-7) and Virginia (20-14) to open the season. Our third game would be the first Saturday in October when the Fightin' Tigers visited Atlanta to play the Georgia Tech Yellow Jackets. The week leading up to the game, I had been working on a stunt at night in

Death Valley. During the game, I was hoisted onto the crossbar of the goal post by the cheerleaders. Before you knew it, there I was walking across the horizontal bar. I made it all the way across without falling.

It was well known that the Georgia Tech fraternity pledges had a bounty on my Tiger tail. After the game, I was chased by the pledges but I beat them to our dressing room and the safety of our football players. I had been given a heads-up by a Tech cheerleader, so I knew I needed to get off the field quickly.

On Monday after the game, I had a note in my mail box from Dean Walter Cox. The note threatened me to within an inch of my life if I ever did that stunt again. It was the one and only time I was on the crossbar.

Final Score: Georgia Tech 38 Clemson 6

JOHN "ZEKE" WELBORN
No. 1 Tiger 1966-67
Bachelor of Science in Civil Engineering '66
Land Surveyor
John H. Welborn Surveyor Inspections & Appraisals
Residence - Greenwood, S.C.
Hometown - Ninety Six, S.C.

Hollywood came to Winston-Salem, N.C. for Wake Forest's 1964 Homecoming game against Clemson and I was the substitute Tiger.

Wake Forest had a pre-game parade on Saturday morning and riding in a Mercedes-Benz convertible was the legendary actress Jayne Mansfield. If you never heard of her, I suggest you Google her. She had the beauty of Marilyn Monroe and it was only fitting for me to do a meet and greet.

This Tiger did everything he could to get inside that convertible; however, she did everything she could to keep me out. As much as I would like to say I was sitting next to her as her leading man in the parade, the fairy tale with the beautiful actress never came to fruition. My attempt, though, has become a legendary story that is told on a regular basis during football season.

Final Score: Clemson 21 Wake Forest 2

In 1966 I dressed before the football games in the newly renamed Fike (Clemson) Field House and signed autographs as I walked towards Memorial Stadium. The Tigers were the defending ACC Champions. Excitement was high on campus as the Tigers opened the season with a 40-35 win over the Virginia Cavaliers. Even more exciting was when the student body tried to pass my 6'8" frame up the stands during the season.

Week two of the football season saw the Tigers head to Atlanta to play Georgia Tech. Coach Howard was a huge figure on campus and getting to be near him was pure pleasure. Prior to the game, I had the opportunity to listen to his pre-game speech to the team. It was legendary, just like our head coach; however, as motivational and funny as it was, the censors won't let me write about it. Catch up with me in Greenwood if you want to hear the story. The Tigers lost to the nationally ranked Yellow Jackets on this Saturday. At years' end, the Tigers had leaped over the Jackets in the conference standings to win their second consecutive ACC Championship.

Final Score: #9 Georgia Tech 13 Clemson 12

ROBERT "POSSUM" HARRIS
No. 1 Tiger 1967-68
Bachelor of Science in Civil Engineering '68
Master of Business Administration '86
University of Richmond
President
Virginia Inspections and Engineering
Residence - Midlothian, Va.
Hometown - Atlanta, Ga.

My first game in the suit was in 1967 when the Tigers hosted Wake Forest. John Enslen, a cheerleader, helped me get up on the crossbar of the goal post. There I was standing proud in front of 36,000 fans when, whap, zing!–someone hit me in the leg with a rock. I didn't last very long up there after getting hit. I got down and prowled the sidelines for the rest of the game as the Tigers won their fourth consecutive home opener.

Final Score: Clemson 23 Wake Forest 6

From 1954 to 1972, Clemson had a student dressed up and known as the Country Gentleman. Butch Roche was the Country Gentleman in 1967. He carried a cane and pushed around a cannon with 10-gauge shells. I told Butch that even though the cannon fired blank shells, it could still be dangerous if pointed at someone. I was standing next to Butch for the opening kickoff to the game. It was a huge mistake. He shot me in the rear. I felt the combustion of the air hitting my suit, plus I could not hear for two days. It was the last time I stood next to or in front of Butch and the cannon.

In week two, we were playing Georgia in Death Valley. I had gone to Athens High School in Athens, Ga. so I was psyched for this game. During halftime, as I looked out at the University of Georgia band, I saw one of my high school girlfriends waving a flag. I slowly crept up on her, grabbed her, and laid her back in a big embrace. (It was the same embrace that you saw growing up watching our military returning home to a hero's welcome in Times Square in the 1940s.) She nearly killed me with the flag pole, but it was worth it.

Final Score: #5 Georgia 24 Clemson 17

During the year, Goody Thomas of Rock Hill provided a car for the cheerleaders to use during the team's entrance, similar to the car used at Georgia Tech today. Goody's son, Craig ("Zero"), was a member of the freshmen cheerleading squad. On this hot afternoon, I was on top of the car with my elbows resting on the crossbar of the goal post. A few seconds later, the cannon fired and the car shot out from under me. I was left hanging for the next few minutes until all of the players had passed under me. My buddies, including Jimmy Addison, the star quarterback, tugged on my tail for good luck. Addison had been named the National Player of the Week for his performance in a 40-35 win over Virginia the previous year. Later that afternoon, I walked off the field having signed more autographs than Addison.

Going into our fourth game of the season, we were 1-2 and playing at Auburn where they had a live eagle as a mascot. Their handlers asked that I hold the War Eagle for a photo. I couldn't act afraid with that big bird on my arm; however, I was scared to death. At day's end, it was our third consecutive loss.

Final Score: Auburn 43   Clemson 21

It was the seventh game of the season and we were undefeated in conference play with a 2-0 record. We were at Chapel Hill, N.C. The dumbest thing I ever did was about to happen. Like any other male, I always tried to impress the ladies, especially from another school. I started talking to a female North Carolina cheerleader. The next thing I knew, I was standing there minus The Tiger head. She had tossed it into the North Carolina stands.

What could my fellow cheerleaders and I do to get the head back? The answer was simple. We kidnapped their mascot, a live goat. A couple of minutes later, we met at midfield and made a trade. That was the last time I ever let anyone hold the head.

Final Score: Clemson 17   North Carolina 0

It was a tradition for us to go over and meet the other team's cheerleaders. This game was at home against NC State. I carried a toilet plunger and my tail had a weight in it which caused it to fly up between my legs when I ran too hard. The wolf, Mr. Wuf, came up to me with his New Jersey accent and told me that he knew karate. I told him that if he tried to karate me, I'd hit him with my plunger.

At halftime, some NC State fans ran onto the field with a big banner that was derogatory towards Clemson. It was high school senior day and the boys in their best Sunday suits were allowed to sit down on the field. I hollered, "We ain't gonna take that. Get em!" and the bleachers emptied. I caught Mr. Wuf out of the corner of my eye coming towards me. A high school player got to him first and hit him right below the knees to flip him in the air. He got up on all fours in time for the Country Gentleman to hit him in the snout, knocking his head off. Two more blows to the back of his real head with his cane and the confrontation was over.

Final Score: Clemson 14 #10 NC State 6

Being The Tiger was dangerous back in the old days. Regardless, I hope the rest of my fellow mascots had as good a time as I did. I still get introduced as the Clemson Tiger and everybody thinks it was a great honor. I don't tell them any different.

ROBERT C. "BOB" DOTSON
No. 1 Tiger 1968-69
Bachelor of Science in Construction Science '71
Human Resources Director
Clayton County Community Services Authority
Residence - Fayetteville, Ga.
Hometown - Atlanta, Ga.

We all talk about how hot it is wearing the suit. After your first appearance you look for ways to stay cool. There were no dri-fit clothes that the students wear today to absorb your sweat. There was no cooling system under the headgear. Nothing. My solution, like other Tigers, was to re-move my t-shirt and gym shorts, leaving just my skivvies on.

Tuscaloosa, Alabama is the home of the University of Alabama. They are very proud of their marching band. As the band took the field, the an-nouncer, in loud, boxing-match style of cadence announced: "And now, Ladies and Gentlemen, the University of Alabama's Million Dollar Crim-son Tide Marching Band!" Which of course was greeted with a standing ovation and cheering from the capacity crowd.

Anyway, the band was huge. When they finally got onto the field for their halftime performance, I was watching and it struck me that they might need help. Understand, that like all of the cheerleading squad, I had in-dulged in a few "adult beverages" prior to the game.

I had gotten into the habit of carrying around on the field a bathroom plunger (yeah the stick with the rubber thing on the end that you use to unclog drains). Well, I decided to take the field with the band, plunger in hand, and proceeded to weave myself in and out of their formations a few times, directing the cadence with my bathroom plunger held high. I am not sure, but I think there were a few boos from the stands, but I did not stay long, so it was probably not about me, although I thought at the time that my performance enhanced their halftime precision.

Anyways, the following Monday I was asked to visit the Dean of Men's office. He told me that the president of the University of Alabama had given him a call and reported that I had "disrupted" their halftime performance. I was told that when we traveled, The Tiger was a symbol of the university and that the university expected such to behave with courtesy, dignity and respect, and that I was to conduct myself like a fine Clemson gentleman. I thought that was what I did, but since the admonition was coupled with a threat of expulsion from the school, I pulled my forelock, apologized, bowed and said it would never happen again.

Final Score: Alabama 21 Clemson 14

In 1967, Mr. Wuf, the NC State mascot, was at the center of the field at Clemson, I think before the game but it might have been at half-time. He had his back to the Clemson sideline. A large number of Clemson stu-dents leaped the wall and attacked Mr. Wuf from behind, throwing him to the ground and tearing his tail.

When the next year was upon us, I heard rumors that when The Tiger got to NC State, the State fans were going to get their revenge. On the way to the game, a supporter of NC State tried to wrestle The Tiger head from me. A struggle ensued and I ended up punching the guy to the ground. I was surprised that no complaint was lodged. That's a first, someone not complaining about what a mascot had done.

I tried to stay as close to the team as possible that day. Prior to the game, the television announcers were introducing the players (who were running to the camera, stopping, being announced and then running off). The players ran to the camera from a position under one of the goal posts. Next, you see Mr. Wuf begin to climb the goal post and stand on the crossbar. The head cheerleader for our squad saw him climbing, and grabbed me and said: "You can't let Mr. Wuf outdo The Tiger." So, up I went. I wasn't sure at the time how high that crossbar was, but it is not easy to shimmy up that pole in a Tiger outfit. As I tried to climb, Mr. Wuf got to the crossbar first and began shaking the goal post. He nearly shook me free from my grasp a number of times as I climbed, so that made the climb that much higher. By the time I got upright on the crossbar, if I could have walked across it to the other side, Mr. Wuf would have gotten another thrashing. Anyway, the television cameras got the players' introduction with mascots in the background.

Final Score: Clemson 24   NC State 19

DOUG PRIDGEON
Freshman Tiger 1968-69
Bachelor of Arts in Sociology '72
Wofford College
Financial Consultant
Cornerstone Wealth and Tax Advisory Group
Residence and Hometown - Spartanburg, S.C.

The freshman football team played their games on Thursdays in Memorial Stadium with less than 10,000 people in attendance. The exception was the one time when we played Duke in the rain at the current Historic Riggs Field/Dr. I.M. Ibrahim Soccer Stadium.

The pep rallies on Friday nights prior to Saturday football games ended with the male cheerleaders and me (The Tiger) getting thrown into the library pool, if the freshmen students (known as Rats) could catch us. One pep rally grew into a panty raid and a Rat riot with dumpsters in downtown Clemson being lit on fire. City and campus police had to come and break it up.

Meanwhile freshmen male students were climbing up on the ledges of Manning Hall to begin their panty raid. Not to be outdone, the freshmen girls reciprocated by holding a jock strap raid on the Tin Cans (Johnstone Hall dormitory) shortly thereafter.

Some of the games lacked action, giving us not enough to cheer about, so we persuaded the cannoneer to shoot the cannon after a good tackle. It quickly ended with a severe tongue-lashing by the coaches and referees.

Although I finished my education at Wofford College, Clemson and being the freshman Tiger will always hold a special place in my heart.

Go Tigers!

SAM COKER
No. 1 Tiger 1969-70
Bachelor of Science in Forestry '72
Owner
South Carolina Pole and Piling
Residence - Gilbert, S.C.
Hometown - Greenville, S.C.

There was a freshman and a varsity Tiger in the 60s. I was the freshman mascot in 1967. I worked the freshman football games and assisted the varsity Tiger, Bob "Possum" Harris. He allowed me to work two pep rallies that year.

The highlight of the year was being the varsity Tiger for a home game against Alabama and Coach Paul "Bear" Bryant. The game was held in Memorial Stadium in front of the largest crowd (49,500) ever at the time in Death Valley. The Alabama quarterback was Ken Stabler, who later became known as "The Snake."

Final Score: Alabama 13   Clemson 10

After several expansions in 1978 and 1983, Memorial Stadium's official attendance increased to 81,500. This mark has been exceeded more than 70 times with the largest crowd (86,092) for Bowden Bowl I on October 23, 1999.

What is interesting about the Memorial Stadium of today is that it is the 16th largest on-campus stadium in the country, second only to Florida State's Doak-Campbell Stadium (82,300) in the ACC. Not bad for a community of approximately 14,000 residents. "There's Something in These Hills" to be able to fill this stadium on football Saturdays.

Due to academic problems, I decided not to try out to be The Tiger the next year. After getting my academics in order, I was back in the suit for the 1969 football season. One of my questions during the interview process of the tryout was how I would help with crowd control and keep events peaceful. My thought was, why do you need a mascot if you want everything to be peaceful? Mascots are motivators, playful characters who interact with and encourage the fans to make noise for their respective team. In the early years, it was interesting at games because visiting fans always wanted to remove my head or take my tail.

Every football season has special memories. The game against Georgia Tech hadn't even started when I saw a Georgia Tech band member place a Clemson football in his tuba. I walked over to the tuba player, placed my arm inside his instrument, and retrieved our game ball. Later that day, the Tigers would get that elusive win on the road. It was Clemson's first win at Georgia Tech since 1945.

Final Score: Clemson 21   Georgia Tech 10

We did not know that the South Carolina game would be Coach Frank Howard's final game prior to his retirement. Coach Howard had prowled the Clemson sideline since 1940. His teams had 165 wins, including an undefeated 11-0 season in 1948, seven outright conference titles, one co-championship conference title, and six bowl trips. Near the end of the South Carolina game, the Country Gentleman (Jim Douglas '70) and I held up a sign at Carolina Stadium wishing South Carolina good luck in the Peach Bowl. In his post-game press conference, the then-South Carolina Head Coach Paul Dietzel appreciated our act of good sportsmanship.

Final Score: South Carolina 27   Clemson 13

CHAPTER THREE
THE 1970s

RANDOLPH DUNBAR JONES JACKSON
No. 1 Tiger 1970-72
Bachelor of Science in Political Science '73
Master of English '75
Hometown - Camden, SC
Deceased 1994

After graduating from Clemson, Randy Jackson became a professor of English at Brevard College in Brevard, N.C. Randy was originally diagnosed with non-Hodgkin's Lymphoma-an Aden carcinoma in December 1981 over Christmas break and was told he had very little time to live. After a 13-year battle against cancer, Randy passed away in 1994.

His son, Joe, shared a few stories about Randy's life as The Tiger in a 2005 Father's Day article on *Tigernet*:

Randy entered Clemson in the fall of 1969 as all freshmen did... as a Rat. The Clemson freshmen were required to wear beanie hats over a shaved head and pretty much memorize the "rat pact." Randy went through the usual motions and made it through his first year without incident.

After Randy's freshman year, he knew he wanted to be a real part of Clemson. He wasn't satisfied with just being part of the crowd, but wanted to do something special. He was already hooked on Clemson football, and being a player wasn't an option. So he did the next best thing. He became The Tiger.

I'm assuming most of you have never worn The Tiger suit... If you have, you can attest that it was not made for hot weather. When Randy was The Tiger, he wore the older version of the Clemson Tiger suit. It wasn't until the year after he was The Tiger that they switched to a new, more modern looking suit.

During the Jackson years, The Tiger didn't do pushups after touchdowns. Instead, on occasion, Dad would climb the goal post and release balloons. In 100-degree weather, this can be as daunting a task as today's pushups. To alleviate some of the heat, I was told that on occasion, an ice-cold fifth of whiskey was taped just below the neck hole on the inside of the

Tiger suit. Randy never got drunk, and rarely buzzed, because of the intense heat and sweat, but the alcohol was enough to take his mind off the heat during some games.

A funny story my granny, Sidney J. Jackson, likes to tell happened in 1971 when Clemson traveled to Auburn. During the pre-game coin flip, Auburn's Head Coach Ralph "Shug" Jordan said to my father, "Hello Randolph, glad to see you again," while Randy was in full Tiger uniform. Baffled and confused, Randy was speechless and just nodded. As it turns out, Coach "Shug" was a good friend of Randy's uncle and had been informed that Randy was The Tiger. Needless to say, being on the road in a hostile environment, Jackson wasn't expecting someone to call him by his name while fully dressed out.

Final Score: #5 Auburn 35   Clemson 13

Randy would remove the head to celebrate scores during games. Below is a great example in *The Daily Item* newspaper in Sumter after his final football game as The Tiger at the Clemson-South Carolina game in Columbia in 1971.

Final Score: Clemson 17   South Carolina 7

Jackson was respected as The Tiger and remained a relative unknown, even though he celebrated with his head off. After his two years as The Tiger, he was offered the opportunity to be Clemson's head cheerleader and take the leadership position. Randy agreed graciously.

In 1972, Randy had the privilege of traveling to Norman, Okla. as the head cheerleader. On many of these football road trips, The Tiger was constantly ridiculed and taunted by opposing fans. This seems to come with the territory with the visiting team. Randy is pictured with The Tiger, Mike Hunt, on the next page.

Final Score: #2 Oklahoma 52   Clemson 3

To say the least, my dad was a character. Family members tell me I got my sense of humor from him, and I don't think I've ever met anyone who could entertain as well. This was his greatest gift. He also possessed the gift of sarcasm. This was not as well received during my father's time as the head cheerleader. He received a lot of compliments; however, he also received a lot of critzcism.

George Bennett, former Clemson head cheerleader and executive director of IPTAY, told me once when I was a child, "Your father, Randy, really shook things up. He was probably the best we had ever had." I'll never forget that. Nor will I forget the hundreds of other people I've bumped into who either personally knew or knew of my dad from his Clemson days. They always had something nice to say.

Through all the criticism and praise, my father stood up for what he believed in, and he believed in Clemson!

Randy had uncontrollable stomach pains, and after diagnosis, doctors performed exploratory surgery on him. At the time, there was no successful form of cancer treatment. There was, however, an experimental treatment at Emory University Hospital in Atlanta that presented a small chance of eliminating his cancer. When you have cancer, any chance is a glimmer of hope.

Almost 14 years later, after hundreds of tumors and countless chemo sessions, lymphoma finally beat my father, Randolph Dunbar Jones Jackson. There is no bigger hero in my life than my father, and every minute of every day, I know that my father was a hero to many others.

He changed lives with his humor, in his teachings at Brevard, he inspired others with his writing, and he encouraged others with his cheers at Clemson. My father left us too early. He probably would have fit in nicely on *Tigernet* today.

Any man can get cancer, but not just "any man" will fight it!

Any man can get called names and put down, but not just any man will stand firm for people they love!

Any man can be funny and make others laugh, but not just any man can change your life.

Any man can have a child, but it takes more than just any man to be a daddy.

Not just any man will carry on when they are faced with defeat or trying times.

MIKE HUNT
No.1 Tiger 1972-74
Bachelor of Science in
*   Parks, Recreation and Tourism '74*
Retired from S.C. Department of Parks,
*   Recreation and Tourism*
Residence - Lexington, S.C.
Hometown - Pickens, S.C.

My Johnstone Hall dormitory supervisor was Carlos Quintero, a varsity cheerleader, who encouraged me to try out for the freshmen cheerleading squad in 1970. He said it was a great way to meet girls and attend all the games. Fortunately, I made the freshman squad.

In 1971, I tried out and made the varsity squad as a line cheerleader. The next year, I became The Tiger. There was a newly designed Tiger suit coming, so I was on cloud nine.

It was the first time anyone would see the new suit, created by a New York costume designer. In my mind, it was the introduction of the current Tiger mascot. The Clemson Tiger was above and beyond the other mascots, especially in the ACC. There were many schools that didn't even have a student mascot. We did it the right way and it was great!

At the time there were no rules about how to wear the suit. The one thing I noticed in previous years was that mascots didn't always wear the head. I think the main reason was because it was so difficult to see how to walk around. I genuinely loved the suit, especially the head, and always kept it on unless I was asked by the administration or someone taking pictures to remove it.

No one likes rats. However, in the military south, freshmen students used to wear a beanie hat at all times and came to be known as "Rats." The Rats at Georgia Tech were like the pesky rodents that try to get into your home. In October 1972 at Bobby Dodd Stadium, these rodents were instructed to retrieve my tail. Signs offered free beer to anyone who could make it happen.

Georgia Tech's precursor mascot to Buzz wandered out on the field. He looked like he was in black footy pajamas with a yellow inflatable stinger sewn to his behind.

He motioned for the Country Gentleman, David Vaughn, and me to come over to him. I was perched on the crossbar of the goal post at the time. It was too tempting not to go, so we went down to meet him. We started pushing each other around. David maneuvered behind him and knelt down as I pushed him over. He hit the ground as the Tech football team was running out on to the field followed by 25 to 30 Rats. As we moved towards our sideline, I got knocked to the ground, and they stole my tail. I picked myself up as Lee Proctor (now a prominent doctor in Conway) led the cheerleaders in a charge to my rescue. I saw one of the Rat's eyeglasses go flying in the air. Lee retrieved the tail and held it up for everybody to see. The tail was taken back just as quickly as it was snatched off.

Several Rats were then handcuffed and led off by Georgia state troopers. We then learned that the president of Georgia Tech had called Clemson President Dr. R.C. Edwards and asked that he not send The Tiger to the game. They had suspected this was going to happen. Thank goodness Dr. Edwards let us go even though I was not made aware of the warning.

Final Score: Georgia Tech 31 Clemson 9

A year later, Dr. Edwards got a similar call from Tech's president pleading, "Don't send the mascot!" Dr. Edwards said no, The Tiger would be there. The freshmen football team, dressed in coat and tie, were my protective escort. It was clear to all but about 10 Rats, who charged the field and were quickly cuffed and carried off to jail.

Final Score: Georgia Tech 29   Clemson 21

During my two years as The Tiger, the cheerleaders and I did several commercials for Hardee's, a long-time sponsor of Clemson Athletics. Each time we got free hamburgers and fries for appearing in the commercial. It was an enjoyable experience for this hungry mascot and his fellow cheerleaders.

On the morning of the Homecoming football game in 1973, I was picked up by the personal chauffeur of Jerry Richardson, owner of Hardee's and later the Carolina Panthers, in Mr. Richardson's Roll Royce. He told me he would take me anywhere I wanted to go around campus or in Clemson.

People would stare at the limo because you never saw anything like that in Clemson. Every so often, we would stop.   The chauffer would walk around to my door, open it, and The Tiger would step out to the surprise of  the fans. Just before kickoff, he drove me straight to midfield of Frank Howard Field inside Memorial Stadium for a grand entrance. It was definitely impressive!

Final Score: Clemson 32   Virginia 27

One time, going to a basketball game from my parents' home in Pickens, I forgot I had placed the head on the roof of my car. As I backed down the driveway, the head rolled off the roof and under the car. I almost had a heart attack because I knew I had run over it. Now I loved the head, and up to that point, I had guarded the new Tiger suit like it was my own child. How could I have done this? When I got out and looked under the car, I saw the head had escaped injury. What a relief!

The question I'm most often asked is about the pushups. I was a "pre-pushups" Tiger. But this has grown to be a very popular tradition for The Tiger. All former mascots watch the current mascots. It's a part of our DNA. The current Tigers are way ahead of us old-timers with their props. However, we always had a rubber chicken or a toilet plunger when playing South Carolina.

I miss the Model A Ford that I got to ride in with the cheerleaders. I've always wondered what happened to it until I found out during the writing of this book. It was sold by Cole Thomas, Zero Thomas's daughter. That car was a great prop for the mascot and cheerleaders.

My dad Woody graduated from Clemson in 1944, my sister Jean in 1975, and my twin sons Coleman and Edward were 2015 graduates. We are surely a Clemson family. As well as continuing a great Clemson legacy, some of my best memories come from my days as The Tiger. Even today, being The Tiger is still a great ice-breaker/door-opener.

TONY SAAD
No. 1 Tiger 1974-76
Bachelor of Science in Textile Science '77
Owner
Industrial Bonded Warehouse
Residence and Hometown - Anderson, S.C.

My first experience in the suit was in September 1974 at College Station, Texas, home to Texas A&M. It was a true honor considering the military history both schools shared. During World War II, Clemson was the non-military instituition that had the second most officers (376) killed in the war. A&M, unfortunately, had a greater loss of life.

The game wasn't very exciting since we lost to the Aggies for the second consecutive year. After the game, I was jumped on the field by several A&M students. They tackled me, ripped The Tiger head off, and went running towards the exit. Little did they know that a future NFL first round draft pick and Super Bowl champion tight end, Benny Cunningham, was still on the field and saw what was happening to his Tiger. He chased down the student with the head and politely made him give it back. I wonder how influential he was. It didn't seem to take much convincing for the student to give up the head.

Final Score: #20 Texas A&M 24   Clemson 0

After two road losses, we returned home and life turned for the better. I often rode a moped with my suit on around the parking lots before games

to hit as many tailgating spots as possible. I quickly learned who had the best food and the best drink. Thank you to those who have ever fed one of the mascots. A poor college student appreciates your hospitality.  But after tailgating, it was time to get to work.

A couple of days prior to the Georgia Tech game, I found a toilet from a building on campus that was being demolished. Needing a prop, I took it and used it at mid-field before the game to sit and read the newspaper. When I was finished with the paper, I jumped up and pulled a stuffed Yellow Jacket out of the "throne."

Final Score: Clemson 21 Georgia Tech 17

With a win over Georgia the next weekend, the Tigers finally owned the state of Georgia with back-to-back wins. It was the first time in 26 attempts over a 68-year span to accomplish this feat.

Final Score: Clemson 28 Georgia 24

My moped days quickly came to an end at the final home game when we hosted the chickens. Somebody let a live rooster on the field before the game, and I chased it with the moped. This ended with a reprimand by the administration. Sure am glad PETA was not around back in the '70s.

Final Score: Clemson 39 South Carolina 21

During the 1974-75 men's basketball season, I witnessed from the floor of Littlejohn Coliseum the play of Wayne "Tree" Rollins and Skip Wise as they beat No. 3 Maryland (83-82), and No. 10 North Carolina (80-72).

Then the 16th ranked Tigers went on to defeat No. 4 NC State (92-70) with their star player, David Thompson.

The second game of the 1975 football season was at the University of Alabama. I went down on the newly named Bryant-Denny Stadium field before the game as the teams were warming up. I made it a point to introduce myself to legendary Head Coach "Bear" Bryant. I remember telling him that I had never met a living legend. He was very pleasant, shook my hand, and asked where I was from. I said, "Anderson, S.C." He then asked if it got hot in that suit. I said, "Well, coach, it does get warm. It's not quite as warm when we win, but it seems to get hotter when we lose." He smiled and said, "Well, you are going to get damn hot tonight." He was right. The Alabama game was a great memory, even in defeat. It's something I still laugh about today.

Final Score: #14 Alabama 56   Clemson 0

After two years wearing the suit, I became the mic man in 1976. It was a very difficult job considering the team went 3-6-2. The underdog Tigers beat the Gamecocks in the final game of the year, and it was fun talking trash throughout that game. This was Coach Red Parker's final game at the helm for the Tigers.

Final Score: Clemson 28   South Carolina 9

As I look back, I am amazed at how many people remember that I was The Tiger. Thank you to all the Tiger faithful. It was a fun experience that I will never forget. I'm glad you haven't forgotten what the mascots were able to get away with prior to all the sportsmanship rules mascots must

abide by today. It was neat getting to sit on the cross bar before some of the games waiting on the team to run down The Hill. It gave a bird's eye view of "The Most Exciting 25 Seconds in College Football," as coined by television announcer Brent Musburger.

GEORGE LANGSTAFF
No. 1 Tiger 1976 (Football Season)
Bachelor of Science in Mechanical Engineering '78
Co-Owner
Shore Things
Residence - Neptune Beach, Fla.
Hometown - Kingsport, Tenn.

My career started as a cheerleader in 1975. Then I switched to being The Tiger for the 1976-77 school year and returned to be the head cheerleader and mic man my last year.

Usually when someone got called to the commandant of cadets during Clemson's military years (1889-1963), they were in trouble. By the time I came along, the college had become a university (1964), and students were sent to the Dean of Students' Office for discipline. When I went to the dean's office, it was to get the suit that was stored in a bass drum case. It had been cleaned, but I remember it being very heavy to wear, and it was hard to see through the nostrils of the head. It was like wearing a giant rug.

The smell became worse as the season went on and the sweat layers soaked into the suit. The best description I can give you would be to imag-

ine yourself locked up in a small space with piles of old sweaty gym clothes surrounding you. Now, I know what my mom went through picking up my clothes when I was growing up. Sorry, Mom!

The only way to care for the suit was to air it out at the apartment and occasionally have it dry cleaned. I remember

Nancy Sasser, then my girlfriend and my wife since 1977, wanted me to take a shower as soon as I could after a game. Understandably. They say humans are attracted to each other by each other's scent. So Nancy, which scent attracted you to me? Pre- or post-shower?

The Tiger suit has been used for many Tigerama skits since 1956. (Tigerama is the annual pep rally put on by the Blue Key Honor Society that is held the evening before the Homecoming football game each year.) I recall being in a skit as we spoofed Mel Brooks's movie "Young Frankenstein."

My most memorable time in the suit away from campus was in Greenville when Coach Howard was being roasted at a fundraiser. In attendance was Coach "Bear" Bryant. Coach Howard was a 1931 graduate of Alabama where he was a star lineman on their January 1, 1931 Rose Bowl team.

DAVID BAIRD
No. 1 Tiger 1976-77 (Basketball Season)
Bachelor of Science in Animal Science '77
Doctor of Medicine '86
Medical University of South Carolina
Practice of General Surgery
Surgical Associates of Charleston
Residence - Charleston, S.C.
Hometown - Darlington, S.C.

The cannon was kept in my room for three years (1974-76). I must admit it came in handy on several occasions. They would put us in jail today for some things we did, so I hope the statute of limitations has expired. The porch roof of Wannamaker Hall was an excellent location to fire the cannon after some successful "streaking," climbing the steps to the fraternity quad in Guy Hendrix's Bronco, and a variety of other events. We even fired it to finish off some really good parties.

There I was standing on The Hill in 1974 prior to our home opener against Georgia Tech. It was the first time I was able to fire the cannon in front of the Clemson faithful and a television audience. Looking across the field, I could see the players exit the locker room to board the bus. A couple of minutes passed and I suddenly heard the roar of the crowd as the buses pull up to the east end zone. As the players unloaded to touch The Rock, Tiger Band began to form the tunnel. It was show time, all I had to do was pull the cord to the cannon to set everything in motion.

On cue, I pulled the cord. Nothing. I quickly pulled again and the result was the same. Nothing. I knew I put the shell in the cannon. How hard could this be? Just pull the cord. There was no third time pulling the cord. It was time to run and get out of the way of the team. Maybe

I should have taken the box of shells and rubbed them on The Rock. Once the game started, I figured out how hard to pull the cord to make it fire.

Shooting the cannon put you in the game without actually playing. Until the mid-90s, we shot the cannon on the same end of the field the Tigers were heading to score. This put you next to the action all the way towards the end zone. I was very careful to be in the clear when I pulled the cord to fire it, and luckily, never received any complaints. Well, almost never. Today, the cannon is on the opposite end of the field, away from the direction Clemson is heading, for safety reasons.

The only thing that saved me on that day was a four-yard game-winning pass from Mike O'Cain to Benny Cunningham midway in the fourth quarter.

Final Score: Clemson 21 Georgia Tech 17

At the Georgia game in 1975, I was told on arrival at Sanford Stadium not to shoot the cannon. Their stadium is named after former University of Georgia English professor Dr. Steadman Vincent Sanford. He later became president and chancellor of the University of Georgia. The first time we kicked off, they promptly confiscated the cannon. We found out later that Uga III, the Georgia bulldog mascot, was gun shy. It wasn't my fault the "Dawg" wasn't wearing ear plugs.

Final Score: #19 Georgia 35 Clemson 7

A week after Valentine's Day in 1976, Norm Sloan's nationally ranked NC State Wolfpack basketball team arrived in Tigertown. During the game, Coach Sloan all of a sudden began yelling at me. He thought I had said something to the mother of his superstar, "Clyde the Glide" Austin, who was sitting behind their bench. I hadn't, but the distraction might have helped in the outcome of the game. Coach Sloan must not know that mascots do not talk while in character.

Final Score: Clemson 103   #12 NC State 90

In the final home game of the season, the Tigers set a Littlejohn Coliseum scoring record when they defeated Florida Southern. For the fifth time during the season, the Tigers eclipsed the century mark.

Final Score: Clemson 122   Florida Southern 79

RANDY ADDISON
No. 1 Tiger 1977 (Football Season)
Bachelor of Science in Ceramic Engineering '79
Hometown - Lancaster, S.C.
Deceased 1980

It's always sad when a member of your family is no longer with you. We lost another member of the Clemson Family in 1980 when Randy Addison passed away after an automobile accident. Randy was a great Tiger, a good friend, a Sigma Alpha Epsilon fraternity brother, and my roommate for two years. If Randy was here I'm sure this was one of his best experiences.

During the 1977 and 1981 football seasons a radio announcer in North Carolina offered a bounty of $100 for the tail of the Clemson Tiger. By the time we played Virginia Tech in Blacksburg, VA on October 1, the bounty had grown to either $200 or $400, depending on who you talked to. Hearing about the bounty, Randy took the mascot suit home to his parents' house in Lancaster. He asked his mother, Beulah, if she could add some reinforcements to the base of the tail. She did by using almost an entire spool of carpet thread. We later learned that was about the strongest thread you could find at that time. When he picked the uniform up a few days later, she told him, "Randy, if anyone gets this tail, they're getting you too, because it's not coming off!"

There were no attempts to get the tail for the first three games that season, and we were beginning to think the bounty was just talk. That changed however, at halftime during the Virginia Tech game. It was an overcast day in Blacksburg that Saturday, and by game time, a steady cold rain began to fall. At halftime, the cheerleaders decided to cross the field to find shelter in the tunnel below the home stands. About the time we entered the tunnel, a loud roar erupted from the stands behind us. We turned around, wondering what was happening, when one of our cheerleaders, Aline Crews, ran up and shouted, they have Randy and are trying to get his tail!

Randy was a strong, athletic guy who could handle himself in most situations. Not wanting him to have all the fun, I immediately took off to see what was happening. Running full speed I saw Randy on the far sidelines, fighting to keep his tail from a group of eight to 10 Virginia Tech cadets~all in dress uniform. The cadets had marched down the sidelines pretending to be part of the halftime show. Being The Tiger, Randy decided to march along with them, swinging his tail and clowning around at their expense. The clowning came to a sudden end when one of them yelled, "Now!" He knew he had been set up when they broke rank and surrounded him, each one grabbing for the tail, trying to be the one to collect the bounty.

Randy had the tail pressed against his body, gripping it with both hands, and was twisting and turning, trying to keep them from getting a hand on it. They were all tightly bunched around Randy when I arrived at the ambush site, still in a full sprint, and launched myself on top of the tightly packed group. All the cadets fell to the rain-soaked muddy ground like so many tin soldiers.

At some point Randy's mask got turned halfway around preventing him from seeing. When he felt someone bump and land next to him,

he quickly wrapped his left arm around the person's neck, pulled him down and started punching him repeatedly. I guess Randy was thinking he was Hall of Famer wrestler "Handsome" Harley Race during the Battle Royale. Fortunately, he was wearing the carpet-thick gloves of his uniform, and was also holding the tail in his right hand, so his punches weren't that effective. I know, because the neck he grabbed and the head he punched was mine!

He finally realized it was me, and together we defended the tail from the cadets. It was a true tag team melee until security personnel broke it up. I later heard from our fans it was the best halftime show they had ever seen. And just for the record, no one ever collected the bounty. Rest in Peace, my friend.

– **Chris Carter for Randy Addison**

Final Score: Addison-Carter, winners of the Battle Royal
Clemson 31 Virginia Tech 13

CHRIS CARTER
No. 1 Tiger 1977-78 (Basketball Season)
Bachelor of Science in Animal Science '79
Account Manager
A&D Environmental Services, Inc.
Residence - Lexington, S.C.
Hometown - W. Columbia, S.C.

Randy Addison, the No. 1 Tiger mascot during the 1977 football season, wanted to experience the excitement of being a cheerleader before he graduated so we switched positions during the 1977-78 basketball season. I had a blast being The Tiger, but as any mascot will tell you, nothing compares to being the mascot on Saturdays during football season. That being said, the following stories are about traditions that exist today. With a lot of traditions, the history of when, how, or why they began is sometimes lost to history. Well, not these!

I made the cheerleading squad in the spring of 1977. At our last meeting/practice before breaking for the summer, George Langstaff, our head cheerleader, along with future head cheerleader Joey Erwin, (yeah, I know he goes by "Joe" now!) challenged each of us to come up with a new cheer. I was a former high school jock and Clemson wrestler, so I didn't know a lot about cheering. I accepted their challenge and came up with the idea of the fans spelling CLEMSON around the stadium.

Several things came to mind as the idea began to develop. One, I had never heard of anyone doing this at other schools. Two, I felt it would give every fan in the stadium a chance to get involved in a cheer. Three, and most importantly for our team, I thought it would be a distraction--if only for a few moments--to the opposing team, which could give our team a temporary advantage. After all, isn't that what cheerleaders are supposed to do?

At the end of summer when the squad met, George and Joey reminded us of their challenge. When I explained the cheer, there was some doubt as to whether the fans would know what we were trying to do, and then do it. Several of the girls came up with the idea of putting large orange letters on white poster board. Then the cheerleaders would hold one up in front of each of the seven sections of the stands when it was time to yell. We knew we could get the Student Section to start the cheer by yelling the letter "C," but we really weren't sure about the other sections. Oh ye of little faith! It took only a few starts before the crowd caught on, and after that a new cheer unique to Clemson became a tradition. We brought the letters to the next game but quickly learned we didn't need them.

Doing pushups would become the second tradition that was started during the fall. This is the tradition of having The Tiger do pushups after every score. That's one pushup for every point after every score. It started with a discussion by one of the cheerleaders who had seen the Penn State Nittany Lion mascot do this at a game. OK, so we borrowed the idea from Penn State, but they were not in our conference and we thought it would go over well with our fans. It did, and another tradition was born. Randy Addison was the first Tiger to do pushups during a football game.

Although not nearly as popular as they once were, you still see more than the occasional fan wearing orange overalls to Clemson sporting events. For those of you who weren't around in the mid- to late seventies, white, loose-fitting painter pants were the cool thing to wear. It soon followed that white overalls also came into vogue.

This was the era of coaches Charlie Pell (1977-78) and Danny Ford (1978-89). We were beginning to win a lot of football games and because of that Clemson was starting to get noticed more on the national level. Our arch-rivals in Columbia had always called us a "Cow College." Playing to that image, but still being stylish and making it something uniquely Clemson, the cheerleading squad began wearing orange overalls.

No one had ever seen orange overalls, much less worn them to a game. Well, like the saying goes, "Where there is a will, there is a way!" I remember calling my mother, Jeanette, and asking if it would be possible to dye white overalls Clemson orange. She said yes, and to bring all of them home and she would dye them orange. I believe we purchased our overalls from

Judge Keller's store.

During the following week, and at my mother's direction, my dad, Fred, purchased all the orange RIT fabric dye he could find from Columbia to Sumter, all the way to Florence. I guess there wasn't a huge demand for orange dye at that time, especially in the middle of the state.

Thanks to my mom and dad, and to a cheerleading squad willing to take a fashion risk, a week later we were wearing orange overalls and another tradition was born. By the time school started the next fall, orange overalls were in stock at Mr. Knickerbocker and many other fine Clemson clothiers. Much to our surprise and delight, we began seeing fans wearing them to games. Even The Tiger said he needed a pair! Sixteen years later, the Tiger Cub was introduced to the world wearing a set of purple overalls.

As Paul Harvey used to say, "Now you know...the rest of the story!"

ZACK MILLS
No. 1 Tiger 1978-80
Bachelor of Science in Animal Science '80
Doctor of Veterinary Medicine '82
University of Georgia
Veterinarian
Tiger Tails Animal Hospital
Residence - Duluth, Ga.
Hometown - Greenville, S.C.

My one and only goal was to be The Tiger, even though I was required to try out to be a cheerleader. Clemson students, my advice is try out to be a mascot. Where else do you have the opportunity to be like the legendary silent comedian Harpo Marx?

I was fortunate that both years I was the mascot the university purchased a new suit. The bad thing is they were only dry cleaned once every two or three months. You need a good roommate (like mine, Ben "Benjie" Everett) to put up with the odor of the suit airing out in your living room.

The early 1970s were not good to the Tigers. However, when I came around in '78, the Tigers were back to their football dominance in the ACC. It's easy to be a good Tiger when your sports programs are winning.

The 1978 First Friday Parade was in its fifth year. I got to ride to the pep rally in a jeep with President Edwards. The question is, why did R.C. and I eat three gold fish at the pep rally? The beverage of choice at the time was not Gatorade, so you can imagine how I felt with those goldfish swimming around in my stomach.

Now, what made me think about doing pushups in the end zone the next day? Sounded like a good idea before we kicked off against The Citadel. It was not until late in the game when it became a problem. I pleaded on my knees, with my hands folded, to Coach Charlie Pell not to score another touchdown. Once a good idea quickly became a bad idea having already completed 288 pushups during the game.

Final Score: Clemson 58   The Citadel 3

A week later, I didn't have to worry about doing pushups. The Tigers never crossed the goal line against the Bulldogs. However, I got called into Dean Walter Cox's office on Monday after the game. It seemed that the Georgia band director didn't appreciate me borrowing an instrument from a member of Tiger Band and joining their performance.

Final Score: Georgia 12   #8 Clemson 0

One of my regular routines on game day was being raised to the sky by members of Tiger Band's flag line using their poles. It was a great skit we performed each week, but what's up with the 8 a.m. practice? Not a good time for rehearsal for a dehydrated mascot.

The best road trip of the year was when we traveled to Wake Forest. It was their Homecoming game and in true mascot tradition, it was important that I get a kiss from the queen. Off I went looking for her court so I would have an escort to her Royal Highness. Unfortunately, I don't have a picture with the queen, but I don't seem to be complaining in this picture.

The next day in the *Charlotte Observer*, the recap of the game was about me wearing a military outfit during the game. I stood on the Wake Forest 20-yard line all day long because the Deacons rarely crossed the 50-yard line.

Final Score: #16 Clemson 51 Wake Forest 6

By the end of the regular season, we had won the ACC championship and were ranked 10th in the country when the Gamecocks came to Death Valley. Nothing like getting a bag of chicken feed and throwing it towards our guests. One thing for sure, the chickens liked the feed better than the final score.

Final Score: #10 Clemson 41 South Carolina 23

A month later, we were headed back to the Gator Bowl for the second consecutive year, this time to play Coach Woody Hayes and his Ohio State Buckeyes. I can remember one of the officials telling me to stay away from Coach Hayes. Instead of trying to score field goals, Coach Hayes was greedy and wanted to score touchdowns against what he felt was an inferior Clemson team.

After an interception by Clemson's middle guard Charlie Bauman, who was tackled out of bounds on the Ohio State sideline, Coach Hayes grabbed and struck Bauman in the throat area. This punch would cause his dismissal as head coach by the Ohio State administration. A big win for the Tigers, but no one remembers the score.

Final Score: #7 Clemson 17 #20 Ohio State 15

Everyone liked the pushup idea; however, not on the ground and in the end zone as was done previously. With the help of Tommy Brown, the first-ever pushup board was built for the 1979 season. The original board was made of wood and was held up by the cheerleaders. Today, The Tiger does his pushups on a board made of a lightweight aluminum panel that is hoisted up in the air by cadets from the ROTC Detachments.

Prior to Clemson's first trip to Notre Dame Stadium in South Bend, Ind. in November, Dean Cox called me into his office. He said by no means was I to grab an instrument and join the Notre Dame Band. As television actor Jim Nabors would say when he portrayed "Gomer Pyle," sha-zam, it was about time someone woke up those echoes in South Bend. That's exactly what I did. However, this time Dean Cox never received a letter from the Notre Dame Band director. Everyone enjoyed my performance, except the Gipper, the ghosts of the four horsemen, and Knute Rockne.

Final Score: #14 Clemson 16   Notre Dame 10

New Year's Eve is supposed to be a fun evening; however, when it is 34 degrees and raining, it wasn't for the Tigers and their fans in Fulton County Stadium in Atlanta for the '79 Peach Bowl. Although I was nice and comfortable in my suit, I came up with the idea that it would be fun to wrestle with the two live bears that Baylor had for mascots. The Clemson football team and I both found out that day that Bears are stronger than a Tiger. I went home with a lot of bruises and a sore knee that still bothers me today

Final Score: #19 Baylor 24   #18 Clemson 18

The two years I was The Tiger, we had a very good men's basketball team. The games were fun; however, just like football games, the suit which felt like it was made of carpet, was still hot to wear.

I spent most of my time sliding across the basketball court during time outs and trying to stay out of trouble with Colonel Rick Robbins. The colonel was the academic advisor for the Athletic Department and the advisor for the mascot and cheerleaders.

The colonel was extremely upset with me after Maryland Hall of Fame Coach Charles "Lefty" Driesell pointed at me as the person causing the basket to move due to my leaning against it. Thankfully, there were stabilizing wires from the backboard to the ceiling of Littlejohn Coliseum. This night, the wires were moving due to the building shaking. The student body was jumping up and down during this historic win over the nationally ranked Terrapins. The colonel feared that we would get a technical foul called against us. It was one of the few times I was totally innocent.

Final Score: #16 Clemson 90   #7 Maryland 81

Just like 1965-66 Tiger "Poag" Reid, I went on to become a veterinarian. I opened Tiger Tails Animal Hospital in 2013 in Duluth, Ga., the same year Clemson defeated the Georgia Bulldogs, 38-35. Like any true Clemson fan or alum, I display a Clemson flag in front of my hospital. Win or lose, we always fly the flag. It is great for business. It doesn't hurt that I have The Tiger's tail from the suit hanging in my office. Plus it's a great beginning for the name of the business.

CHAPTER FOUR
THE 1980s

RICKY CAPPS
No. 1 Tiger 1980-82
Bachelor of Science in Agricultural Engineering '82
Vice President
USA Fibre Solutions, Inc.
Residence - Easley, S.C.
Hometown - Hendersonville, N.C.

When I became The Tiger, I had big shoes to fill replacing Zack Mills. The team I was representing was joining Ohio State, Michigan, and Southern Cal (the real USC), just to name a few, as a national football power. I wanted to be the perfect representative for the university, as well as a great entertainer. What better way than being The Tiger? The suit gives you a sense of confidence and a personality that is bigger than your own.

My first appearance was the 1980 First Friday Parade prior to the home opener against Rice. I rode my motorcycle in the parade as The Tiger. The next day, I rode into Death Valley without permission and was banned from riding in the stadium at future games. Today, I see the Demon Deacon leading his team onto the field with a motorcycle and wonder why I had to stop.

Final Score: Clemson 19   Rice 3

We arrived early in Athens, Ga. for the second game of the year having made the 80-mile trip across the state line in two vans with the Clemson University seal on the doors. I had heard about Dawg fans, but thought it was all hype. It wasn't. As we traveled towards the stadium, the fans walking along the streets would yell and taunt us as we passed. In an effort to make an impression, I slipped on the suit, went out the passenger window, and climbed up on top of the van. This was immediately met with loud boos. Empty bottles were being hurled at the van as we passed the infamous train trestle near the stadium. Most missed; however, one damaged our windshield. Enough of riding on top of the van.

Upon arriving at Sanford Stadium, the teams were stretching as the stands were filling up. I made my way on to the field to get a close look at Herschel Walker, the Georgia running back. Herschel was everything they

were writing about him, and in 1982 would win the Heisman Trophy. He looked bigger and more ominous the closer you got to him.

Next was a walk over to the home of Uga, the team's bulldog mascot. As I was petting him, I asked if I could take Uga for a walk. After a few seconds, the person in charge agreed, but said to bring him right back. I set off down the sideline and as time passed, they motioned for me to return. I shook my head, NO. He started after me as I pulled on Uga's leash. Bulldogs don't run very fast, especially in the heat. I was urging him on and eventually seemed to almost drag Uga down the sideline. Georgia fans were booing, and Clemson fans were laughing. Eventually a few angry guards caught up to me and retrieved Uga.

Final Score: #10 Georgia 20   Clemson 16

Prior to the game, I decided to march with the Duke flag corps carrying a Clemson flag. The Clemson fans cheered loudly as I walked up and down the field. Later during the game, I climbed up on the drum major ladder and pretended to direct the Duke band. I didn't realize the real drum major was on the ground looking up at me trying to do his job. On Monday I had to write a letter of apology to the Duke administration.

Final Score: Duke 34 Clemson 17

The last conference game in 1980 was at Maryland. They had a car that looked like a turtle circling the track around their football field. I climbed on top and went for a ride. At the end of the field, there was a net filled with helium balloons to be released prior to kickoff. After I got off the car, I headed to the net with the balloons. I jumped into the net planning to lay there for a while. However, when I jumped, the net came loose and all the balloons floated away. The Maryland fans and administration were not happy.

Final Score: Maryland 34 Clemson 7

The second game in 1981 almost took place without the presence of The Tiger. The cheerleading squad and I traveled the 592 miles to New Orleans, once again in two vans. On the day of the game, David Pinion, a cheerleader, was driving us around New Orleans when we got involved in a fender bender. The New Orleans police were called to the scene. We assumed this would be taken care of at the scene, a minor citation issued, and we would be on our way to the game with plenty of time. As Lee Corso would say, "Not so fast." If you are from out-of-state, you are taken to the police station and bail has to be arranged. I still remember David staring back at me from the back seat of the patrol car with a terrified look on his face as the car drove away. I followed the patrol car to the station. Time was becoming a factor. Bail was set at $50. David and I had $51 between us. With the bail paid, we sped off to the Louisiana Superdome. I changed into the suit as we pulled into the parking lot. As I entered the Superdome, Tiger Band was playing and I got there just in time to lead the Tigers onto the field. That was a close one.

Final Score: Clemson 13 Tulane 5

Anything can happen when you are playing Wake Forest on Halloween in Death Valley. There is no way I can describe what it was like doing push-ups during the game. First, I set the record for the most pushups (175) in the second quarter. Next, before I could finish doing 62 pushups in the third quarter, the Tigers had scored again. This meant I would have to add seven more to the total and begin another set of pushups (69). Finally, there was a memorable moment in the fourth quarter when the Demon

Deacon mascot came to my assistance. The pushups were taking a toll on this Tiger. With a little help from the Demon Deacon, a new record was set for the most pushups in a game (465). This was the first and only time a visiting mascot has ever done pushups to celebrate a Clemson score. My fellow mascot was definitely a first responder to this Tiger in need.

(Here is my take on that fateful Halloween afternoon.
Chris Kibler, WFU Deacon mascot 1981-84)

It was a cloudy day in Death Valley, and it was getting cloudier by the minute as the Clemson Tigers had just scored their 69th point in the fourth quarter. I turned to our mic man, Joe Morrow, and told him that despite the somber mood on our side of the field, I was going to try to brighten things up a bit. As the Deacon mascot, I couldn't help but feel sorry for my fellow partner-in-crime in The Tiger suit on the home team side of the field. He was struggling to keep up with the exponentially growing number of push-ups. So, I thought, if you can't beat 'em, join 'em. I wandered over to the end zone opposite of where the Tigers were heading. When they finally crossed the goal-line again, I ambled over to the Clemson cheerleaders and found a very fatigued Tiger (Ricky Capps) and basically mimed to him and the crowd that I wanted to help him out in his time of need. It would be my honor to perform the 76 pushups for him as a show of good sportsmanship. So they hoisted me up on the board, and I cranked out 76 adrenaline-assisted pushups. The crowd went wild and proceeded to pass both The

Tiger and the Deacon overhead to the top of the lower section of the stadium. Little did I know, but the little show of mascot cooperation would be featured in the college football section of *Sports Illustrated* the next week. That afternoon in Death Valley was certainly one of my most memorable highlights of my three years as the Deacon.

It didn't take long for someone to print a tee shirt with a picture of The Tiger on it with his arms crossed over his head, and the caption reading, "No More Pushups." Just think how tired the mascot would have been in 1901 if there'd even been a Tiger doing pushups when Clemson defeated Guilford 122 to 0 on Bowman Field (Clemson's original football field from 1898 to 1941).

Final Score: #3 Clemson 82   Wake Forest 24

On Monday, I received a phone call from a radio station in Chapel Hill, N.C. The radio personality informed me we were on the air, and that a bounty had been issued by a Tar Heel fraternity for $100 for anyone who would rip the tail from the suit and bring it to the fraternity house. I gave a smart response assuring him that under no circumstance would the tail be torn from the suit. We had a fun exchange and the call ended. The next evening, he called again saying the fraternity had heard the interview and increased the reward to $250. I countered by saying we would add additional security with muscle-bound cheerleaders and a South Carolina highway patrolman to counter such an attack. It was all in fun, and the conversation ended.

On Thursday, I received my final call from the radio station. The disc jockey said the fraternity had again increased the reward, this time to $500 for The Tiger's tail. I went silent and thought for a moment. When asked if I had a response, I told him that I was a poor college student and for $500, I might deliver the tail personally to the fraternity house. The station erupted in laughter. A couple of attempts were made for the tail during the game, but it remained intact, and Clemson went on to win a close game against the Tar Heels.

Final Score: #2 Clemson 10   #8 North Carolina 8

There was no way I could top the experience of total exhaustion at the Wake Forest game, but this was a very special year in Clemson Football.

I was given the honor of dotting the "i" prior to the National Championship game at the 1982 Orange Bowl in Miami. Thank you, Clemson University, and congratulations to Coach Ford and the 1981 football team on winning Clemson's first team championship. At the time, the only other championship had been won by Noel Loban in 1980 as a 190-pound wrestler.

Final Score: #1 Clemson 22   #4 Nebraska 15

My daughter, Taylor, as a junior at Clemson in 2014 was fortunate enough to get a marketing internship with the Athletic Department. The doorbell rang at our house on my birthday in February. I opened the front door and there stood the Tiger Cub holding a sign that read "Happy Birthday Dad." What a great surprise! Not only was the Cub visiting me on my birthday, but it was my daughter. As Clint Eastwood would say, "Make my day." Clemson always finds a special way to take care of family.

RANDY FAILE
No. 1 Tiger 1982-84
Bachelor of Science in Administrative Management '84
Director of Sales
ServTrax
Residence - Atlanta, Ga.
Hometown - Aiken, S.C.

Carol Ratchford was a cheerleader at my high school in Aiken. When she came to Clemson, she wanted to try out for cheerleading. So she asked me to help her with her stunts. When we arrived at the tryout at Fike Field House, there were about 100 beautiful ladies and about 50 or so guys. I liked the odds. I was hooked and was selected for the junior varsity squad.

After a year on the JV squad, I made the varsity squad the next year. The cheerleading squad consisted of six males and six females, a mic man, a cannoneer, and me as The Tiger. Ricky Capps, The Tiger the past two years, was graduating, and he thought I would make a great mascot. Nothing like getting a letter of recommendation from the former mascot who held two pushup records.

Here I was replacing Ricky, and Clemson was the defending national football champion. Not much pressure for a rookie mascot! Off the cheer-

leaders and I went to summer spirit (National Cheerleader Association) camp at Southern Methodist University in Dallas.

During one of the cheerleader routines, I flew through the middle of the formation using a mini trampoline. What would have been a perfect 10 score in gymnastics helped me be named the Mascot of the Year at camp. It was a stunt I would repeat during basketball season completing a full forward flip as I slam-dunked a basketball.

With my own championship in hand, I was ready to open up the home football season against Boston College. It would be my "burning down the house" moment. Dressed in full camouflage gear, I did a skit with a papier-maché eagle borrowed from a First Friday Parade float the previous night.

After Tiger Band's halftime performance, I was poised on the 20-yard line with the cannon and my new papier-maché bird. I started counting to three: one, two and on the count of three, I pulled the cord and fired the cannon toward the eagle. The combustion from the blank shell sent the eagle through the air towards the upright and the end zone. Not quite a field goal, but a pretty good attempt, if you ask me.

After the smoke had cleared, I went to retrieve my prey and began the famous Tiger swagger to the sideline. Before I could make it off the field, the eagle erupted into flames. I suddenly felt like I was on fire. I threw my head off...yes unthinkable...and dropped the burning eagle on the field.

Coach Ford was in his well-known pose on one knee as his players were warming up after the halftime break. His glare towards me almost put out the fire. With some help from those on the sideline, we quickly extinguished the fire. It left a three-foot circle burned on the home side.

Final Score: #16 Clemson 17   Boston College 17

My "chicken on the loose" moment almost got me arrested. I
know it wasn't a red rooster;
however, a chicken is a chicken.
There I was running on the field
with a chicken tied to a rope until
the chicken got loose. Clemson
President Dr. Bill Atchley (1979-
86) phoned down to the field
and told two South Carolina
highway patrolmen to grab me.
I told the officer he wouldn't
make it out of the stadium with
me in handcuffs. Fortunately he
agreed so we were able to get the

chicken back into the coop. Everyone was happy! At least those who were
Clemson fans.

Final Score: #13 Clemson 22   South Carolina 13

Appearances at special events were not as prevalent in the early 1980s as
they are today. However, Beth Cousins (cheerleader and 1983 Homecoming Queen) persuaded me to participate in the Egg and Dairy Festival in
Newberry.

The only regularly scheduled appearance I had was at Calhoun Corners in Clemson. I appeared as The Tiger after each home game to sign autographs, joke with the crowd, and have my picture taken. Afterwards, I was able to enjoy a great meal (complimentary) with my girlfriend Trellise Barden, who worked at the restaurant. She became my wife in 1986.

All the former mascots watch the current Tigers. I can't stress enough how important it is to see an animated figure and not just a person in the suit. This means using huge motions throughout the day from walking to running and especially waving to the crowd. Each gesture or action you make in the suit has to be to the extreme, or you just look like a guy dressed in a suit. We want to see high energy.

As you are constantly reminded, someone is always watching you, especially those in the mascot fraternity.

JAY WATSON
No. 1 Tiger 1984-85
Bachelor of Science in Industrial Management '85
CEO
Forefront Networks, Inc.
3Can Events
Residence - Austin, Texas
Hometown - Greenville, S.C.

President Atchley called and asked if I wanted to attend a re-election rally for the 40th President of the United States, Ronald Wilson Reagan (1981-89) in Greenville, along with members of Tiger Band. That was an easy answer. What an honor!

Upon arrival at the rally, the Secret Service went through every inch of the bag which was holding The Tiger suit. Wearing gym shorts and a tee shirt, I was also given a pat down. From that point on, I had an agent assigned to me and was asked to stay put until they were ready for me. Forty-five minutes later, I was briefed again by a Secret Service officer. My spot on the stage would be adjacent to the podium. I was not allowed to do anything but sit. NO big movements towards the President or I would be pulled off stage. They were very clear this was to be taken seriously.

I had a Clemson baseball hat that I asked if I could give to the President. They said it would be OK, but I had to do it as he walked on the stage.

Once again, I was reminded NO big movements and NO sudden advances towards the President. I took my place on stage with Greenville Mayor Bill Workman and U.S. Congressman Carroll Campbell, Jr. (He would later become the 112th governor of South Carolina). When the President arrived on stage and was close to the podium, I managed to get around all the dignitaries and hand him the hat. He immediately put it on and the crowd went crazy. After a quick handshake, I went back to my seat with my duties now complete–or so I thought.

President Reagan was a former movie actor who played George "The Gipper" Gipp in the 1940 movie "Knute Rockne All-American." The movie is on television every year, mysteriously right before National Signing Day and the beginning of football season.

During the President's seemingly endless speech, I think I might have nodded off a bit, until I got a poke in the back. There is a video that shows my head adjacent to the President suddenly turning around and looking between the curtains behind us. The same Secret Service agent who told me to sit still and not make any sudden movements had given me the nudge. He said, "You need to do your job and get this crowd excited."

So without overthinking the moment, I waited for a chance in which I could stand up and clap. I found that moment, stood up and the crowd responded. I sat down quickly and noticed that the President had no idea that I had stood up. He thought it was his words. He seemed to find some energy and left his monotone delivery and started to get into the moment. I continued to stand and sit, saluting when he made reference to those serving in our Armed Forces, clapping as appropriate and generally getting the crowd into the event. It was an absolute blast. At one point, Reagan acknowledged my antics with a huge smile and a nod. As things wrapped up, I led a "Four More Years" cheer that seemed to go on for five minutes. I finally left the stage, worked the crowd, and found my way back to the bus. All in a day's work. One of the traits of being a mascot is to be spontaneous–but in front of the President of the United States?

Imagine my surprise the next morning when I woke up and saw the *Greenville News* headline "Tiger throws partisan support to Republicans." It was a media storm for the next three days.

Congressman Campbell wrote me a personal letter saying he was sorry for the turmoil, but if there was ever anything he could do for me, to let him know. President Reagan sent me a signed photograph of us together with the Clemson hat in his hand.

President Atchley eventually called me to his office with no fewer than five media trucks and cameramen wanting an interview. We talked baseball, politics, and Clemson for 30 minutes, while the media waited in the lobby. He then asked if I wanted to be interviewed (I had already endured two days of this) and I said, "Not really." He agreed and led me out of Sikes Hall through a back way so I could avoid further questioning. He was great and laughed about it, saying this would certainly make for fun conversation years from now. He was right. How many people get a chance to meet a U.S. President, much less get to be part of his "show"? THAT is the power of The Tiger. Even the President needed the help of a Tiger! My mom made a scrapbook of the photos and articles from this event which we display prominently in our home.

Looking back on this day, what could have been perceived as mocking the President fortunately was a positive game changer for the rally. It is one of the reasons that the mascots today do not attend political appearances.

Since then, I have had a couple of opportunities to spend time with President George Herbert Walker Bush, otherwise known as Bush 41, and we have laughed about this story. I parachuted out of a plane in 1985 and 1986 for stress relief from IBM School. Bush 41 made tandem jumps on his 80th, 85th, and 90th birthdays.

OK, let's get back to how I became The Tiger. Woody Binnicker and I were both on the cheerleading squad. Woody decided he wanted to be the head cheerleader and mic man, and I wanted to be The Tiger.

To be the mascot, you still had to make the cheerleading squad. I always thought this limited the pool of possible candidates so we started a conversation with the administration about getting an independent tryout for those who wanted to be the mascot.

We both made the squad and I became The Tiger. Putting on the suit for the first time was electric, just like my first sky-dive. A rush that was one part euphoria and one part "You'd better not mess up."

Our outside appearances were always optional, but the administrators advised us regarding those that we should "strongly" consider. One of my first appearances was at the Special Olympics. This is still one of my most memorable events. Other memorable events were a ladies luncheon (not for this book), and an alumni fundraiser in Greenville.

My most memorable game day experience started with me walking from my dorm room in Johnstone Hall to the stadium for the first time. It took me 30 minutes to make the hundred-yard walk. I had no idea how many people would stop me for a picture or ask for an autograph. It was everything I had hoped it would be times ten.

After the game started, I was walking on the sideline early in the first quarter getting used to the stadium and where I could go. There did not seem to be any limitations. I decided to stand on the sideline next to Coach Danny Ford. He was in his usual squatted position about the 40-yard line, so I positioned myself about five yards from him in a similar squat, stroking my chin, moving my arms around after a play. Then all of a sudden I hear, "What are you doing here? Get him outta here, now!" A couple of assistant coaches were laughing as they kicked me off the sideline. Pretty funny looking back on it, but I can certainly understand the displeasure Coach Ford showed at the moment. Today there are police officers, strength coaches, assistant coaches, and administrators monitoring everyone on the sideline.

Final Score: #4 Clemson 40 Appalachian State 7

My visit to Scott Stadium in Charlottesville, Va. was a memorable day. The Tigers shut out the Cavaliers and I did 303 pushups. Don't know how Ricky Capps did his 465 against Wake Forest a few years earlier. This feat should be considered legendary.

Final Score: #3 Clemson 55 Virginia 0

Being ranked number two in the country and on top of the world can change quickly. A week later, I was standing under the goal post at Georgia when Kevin Butler kicked the game-winning 60-yard field goal with 11 seconds remaining. The outcome took a toll on everyone. I watched as the ball crossed over the bar with only a couple of yards to spare.

Every table in the locker room after the game had a body on it with an IV in a player's arm. I could not take a step or even sit up without every muscle cramping due to the dehydration. When you fall, you fall fast. The Tigers fell 11 spots in the polls on Monday. After another loss the next week to Georgia Tech (28-21), the Tigers were out of the Top 20.

Final Score: #20 Georgia 26   #2 Clemson 23

Interacting with the student body was always a highlight. During each game, I would walk back and forth on the platform with the mic man. Next thing I know, I was body surfing from the front to the back row of the stands through the Kappa Sig's section to see my date or get a small (sometimes large) dose of bourbon. They would generally drop me in the crowd of brothers, pull my head off, give me a mouthful of something, put my head back on, pick me up and send me off, all in twenty or thirty seconds. It was a blast. Wouldn't dare try that stunt today with cell phones and television cameras everywhere.

Still to this day, most people ask why sitting at a basketball game next to Shawn Weatherly, 1980 Miss Universe, was not my best memory. Wow! She was pretty, nice, and it was the one and only time I really thought about violating the "No Talk Rule."

As I look back, being The Tiger has forever endeared me to the school. It has opened doors, created relationships, and made me laugh for more than thirty years.

DAVID FRIEDMAN
No. 1 Tiger 1985-86
Bachelor of Science in
*   Administration Management '86*
President and Executive Director
Carbon, Inc.
Residence - Folly Beach, S.C.
Hometown - Rock Hill, S.C.

Jay Watson had asked the administration the previous year for a separate mascot tryout and a year later it happened. I was selected as The Tiger. No more being a cheerleader first and then being selected to be the mascot.

Everyone was excited in Clemson as the football program was coming off two years of no televised games due to sanctions by the NCAA. The top CBS announcer, Brent Musburger, would be calling the second game of the season against Georgia. Brent's rival at the time was ABC's Keith "Whoa Nellie" Jackson. It was at this game that Brent coined the phrase "The Most Exciting 25 Seconds in College Football."

The night prior to the game, I hid four large poster-sized cards in Memorial Stadium. The next day, I paraded around during pre-game for over an hour. You are always nervous whenever you are in The Tiger suit because you do not know what the fans actually notice you doing, either intentionally or unintentionally. I had a Crown Royal bag tied tightly to my paw (wrist).

Near the end of the first quarter, I flashed the first cue card towards where my girlfriend was sitting with the the PiKA fraternity in the stands. She was probably thinking, "Oh gosh, what's he getting ready to do?!"

The first card read "Terri Underberg," followed by "WILL" followed by "YOU." By the second card, all the women knew what was happening and were beginning to clap. Conversely, all the guys had a puzzled look (likely alcohol induced), in response to the first two cards. By the third one, I could hear them all screaming "Don't do it!" It was all soon put to rest by the final card: "MARRY ME?"

Then I climbed into the stands, maneuvered up to where she was and in keeping with tradition, put The Tiger snout up to her face. I then asked her in person to be my wife, apologizing that while I wanted to do so, I couldn't take off the head, so I couldn't punctuate it with a kiss. I then untied the Crown Royal bag and handed it to her. It contained her ring! We've been together ever since and have three grown children. We lost the game, but I got the love of my life.

Final Score: Georgia 20   Clemson 13

Clemson is a special place, especially at the end of the game when kids jump over the wall onto the field. After one game, I recall a young girl running eagerly with her arms spread in hopes of being the first to hug The Tiger. She ran full force into me and we hugged. Immediately, she pulled back with a grimacing look and yelled, "Oh gross! I've been slimed!" What a special moment in her life. I'm sure as an adult she still remembers that embrace, along with thousands of other children and adults who have hugged one of the mascots after a long, hot day in the sun.

My engagement made the beginning of the season fantastic. The season, however, was just average for both South Carolina (6-4) and Clemson (5-5) heading into the final game of the year down in Columbia. A win could send you to a bowl game; a loss, you would be heading home for the holidays. The Tigers defeated the Gamecocks 24-17 and were invited to the Independence Bowl in Shreveport, La. to play the Minnesota Golden Gophers. South Carolina went home for the holidays.

Bowl games are usually fun and often unique, especially when playing someone from the Big Ten Conference. Shreveport wasn't nice to the Tigers, as we lost to the Gophers, 20-13. However for this Tiger, it was an honor to meet Marine Lieutenant Clebe McClary, who delivered a moving breakfast speech on his experiences in Vietnam. Lieutenant McClary lost an eye and an arm during a reconnaissance mission. He would later be presented with a Silver Star and a Bronze Star. What a great and honorable man. Ooh Rah!!!

INDEPENDENCE BOWL

My claim to fame was when I hit legendary North Carolina Head Basketball Coach Dean Smith in the nose. At the time, North Carolina was ranked No. 1 in the nation. As the teams were heading to the locker rooms for halftime, I was entering the tunnel when a fan asked me to "slap him five."

Coach Smith wasn't paying attention and was just off my left shoulder when I stopped, planted my feet, and extended my left arm. That's when his "schnoz" and my elbow connected just like a punch in one of the Sugar

Ray Leonard-Roberto Duran fights. It was so forceful, his head went back and he literally thought he had been punched.

I was clueless about what was transpiring until I started feeling girly punches. Coach Smith was punching me. At that point, I instinctively went into "fight mode" not knowing who it was, only that some fool seemed to want some of me. As I drew back to defend myself, the players grabbed me and were yelling, "You're gonna get expelled! What are you doing?" Clearly no one knew at the time that he started it.

Coach Smith refused for a while to continue towards the locker room and instead wanted to fight. The remainder of the game, he kept holding his nose while he yelled at his players on the court. Soon the fans were mocking him by holding their noses. The night ended in a draw.

Final Score: Tiger 1   Schnoz 0
#1 North Carolina 79   Clemson 64

CHRIS SHIMAKONIS
No. 1 Tiger 1986-87
Bachelor of Science in Civil Engineering '88
General Contractor
Coleman Builders
Residence - Mount Pleasant, S.C.
Hometown - Greenwood, S.C.

They posted the names of the 1986-87 cheerleading squad on the outside door of Mell Hall. I walked over before lunch, saw my name, and was super excited! I couldn't wait to get started as The Tiger.

Our annual summer camp was in Memphis, Tenn. After a week of all-day camp and summer heat, the squad was exhausted and ready to return to Clemson. The passengers settled in for a nap in our van, while Luke Lucas and I took over the driving duties. Everyone else was in a deep sleep. We opened the small window vents so Luke and I could get some air, but turned the van heat on maximum and flooded the cabin with super-hot air. A perfect combination for a hot July day. It took five minutes before the group woke up. Everyone was sweating, and some looked like they were ready to cry. If you can't laugh at others, who can you laugh at? Such is the goal of a mascot.

Football season began with an opening loss to Virginia Tech (20-14).

We then traveled to Athens, Ga. to play the Dawgs. It was 88 degrees with 54 percent humidity outside the stadium and probably over 100 degrees on the field. The game ended with David Treadwell's 46-yard field goal going through the uprights as time expired. The Tigers had upset the Dawgs. Following the game, you could see their fans throw some of their relatives (chili dogs) into the air as they were leaving the stadium.

Final Score: Clemson 31   #14 Georgia 28

We had some really fun personalities on our cheerleading squad. Once during a football game, I "borrowed" a tube of lipstick and smeared it on the mouthpiece of John Shelbe's megaphone. After several cheers with the megaphone pressed against his mouth, he finally realized why the fans sitting in the first few rows were laughing. He had a red ring mustache and goatee, similar to the look of comic actor Charlie Chaplin.

My ole buddy Luke never wanted his uniform or hair out of place, just like the mascot after me, Martin Lowry. This often made Luke a target for The Tiger. When it rained during games, The Tiger's tail

would be muddy and soaked with water. With the tail in my hand, I would strike Luke across his back. Then, I would yell to Luke, "You may want to 'Shout' that stain out!" I had ruined his pretty boy looks.

I had a mannequin prop as my Homecoming date for the Duke game. I carried her around with me the entire day. We ran down The Hill together. We did cheerleader stunts together. We even got passed up into the student section. Unfortunately, it got a little out of hand, and I had to apologize to several fans through the Dean of Students' Office the next week.

Final Score: #17 Clemson 35   Duke 3

During the season, a fan gave me a pair of
Tiger Paw boxer shorts and asked me to wear
them for good luck. The timing was just right
during a night game at home against the Tar
Heels. After completing a set of pushups,
I stood up on the pushup board and all of
sudden, there was an orange moon. The students loved it, the dean of student life, not
so much. The stunt landed me in a second
meeting with the dean as The Tiger. I guess it
was no laughing matter.

Final Score: Clemson 38   North Carolina 10

The best skit I ever performed was when I impersonated Coach Ford during the start of the 1986 Maryland game. Due to his conduct the previous year after a 34-31 home loss to Maryland, Coach Ford was suspended
from the field by the ACC officials. He was then allowed to coach from
the press box at Memorial Stadium in Baltimore. The Terrapins would
occasionally play games in the larger stadium (47,855 vs. 34,680) instead
of on campus.

During his weekly press conference, Coach Ford commented to the
media he would be on the field as The Tiger. So I ran out with the team,
spitting tobacco, pacing the sidelines, and imitating Coach Ford. After
about 10 minutes, a CBS representative asked me if they could do a story
on my antics as The Tiger. The answer was yes!

In 2014, I became the interim head football coach at Palmetto Christian Academy. While coaching a game from the sidelines, I got wiped out
on a play, breaking my leg in four places. This caused me to miss the mascot
reunion later that fall. I should had coached from the press box. It's safer
and helped Coach Ford and the Tigers win the first of three consecutive
ACC championships (1986, 1987, and 1988).

Final Score: #15 Clemson 17   Maryland 17

The next weekend in Clemson, the unthinkable happened again for the
fourth and last time while playing South Carolina. When the game ended, 82,492 Clemson and South Carolina football fans left the stadium
speechless. Everyone went to their cars, packed up their tailgates and

headed home wondering how could this happen again? There were no bragging rights!

Final Score: #19 Clemson 21   South Carolina 21

The 1986 season ended in Jacksonville, Fla. with the Tigers playing the Stanford Cardinal in the Gator Bowl. The game was dominated by the Tigers (27-0) in the first half. I couldn't wait to get to the locker room to get out of the suit for a few minutes. Coach Ford greeted me with "You must be exhausted! Here, take mine." He handed me the Coke he had been drinking. That drink reminded me of the 1979 Coca-Cola commercial featuring "Mean" Joe Greene of the Pittsburgh Steelers throwing his jersey to a little boy after a game.

Final Score: #21 Clemson 27   #20 Stanford 20

Cheerleaders and mascots had the opportunity to join the Block C Club as a letterwinner. To become a member of Block C, we had to make a wooden paddle, paint it orange, and get signatures of members on the paddle. The toughest signature to get was Coach Howard's. The end of the week was drawing near so I hung out at the Jervey Athletic Center waiting on Coach Howard to leave. When he finally came out, he asked me where I was from and I said, "Greenwood." Anyone can coach, but to become a legend, you have to tell a great yarn. He immediately went into stories about "Pinky" Babb and Walter Cox. He said back in his early days as a head coach, Clemson was a military college with no girls on campus. He would send his assistant coaches after practice down to the train station to stop players from leaving campus for one of the state co-ed schools. It was truly a highlight for me to listen to this legendary figure.

MARTIN LOWRY
No. 1 Tiger 1987-89
Bachelor of Science in Mechanical Engineering '88
Master of Business Administration '92
President
Thomas Mechanical, Inc.
Residence and Hometown - Laurens, S.C.

What is the meaning of "no show"? It's when someone is advertised to be in attendance and then does not make the appearance. In 1987, that was me. As the new Tiger, I left the hands to the suit in my University Ridge apartment.

When I went back to my apartment to get them, I realized that I had left my keys in the Jervey Athletic Center laundry room. Thank goodness I knew my second-floor sliding glass door was unlocked. Acting like Spiderman, I scaled the brick wall, scraping my knee as I went up and over the railing.

This scrape was actually a laceration to the top of my kneecap. With one hand on my knee, I walked downstairs to get help from some friends—girls, of course. They freaked out when they saw the blood. Instead of going to Redfern Health Center on campus, I calmly told them to take me to Jervey to see the team doctor. Dr. Larry Bowman was the new orthopedic surgeon. After a couple of stitches, the knee ended up being fine, but I have a scar to this day, a reminder of my "no show."

The suit was downright nasty after a football game. In an attempt to make it bearable for a Sunday soccer game, I hung it out the window of my room in the Sigma Alpha Epsilon house to air out overnight. The next day a little girl came up to me and said, "I know where you live." I looked at her and shrugged my shoulders. She said it again, but this time she pointed to my room, which overlooked the soccer field. I shrugged again and she said for a third time, "I know you live up there because I saw you hanging out the window." That little girl had ridden past the soccer field, looked across towards my room, and saw The Tiger hanging out the window. I picked her up and gave her the biggest hug ever.

I was a freshman when Clemson won their first National Soccer Championship in 1984. Three years later, I got to participate in the presentation of the 1987 National Soccer Championship trophy during halftime of a basketball game. The Tigers claimed their second national championship in three years following their 2-0 victory over San Diego State at Historic Riggs Field.

In 1988, I had a CO_2 fire extinguisher as a prop with RAID (the bug killer) written on the side of it so I could spray Buzz, the Georgia Tech student mascot. Instead of spraying Buzz, I sprayed the giant blow-up yellow jacket that stands in the end zone at Georgia Tech. I got away with it two times during the game, but on the third attempt, a security guard came up to me and said, "If you do it one more time, you will be escorted out of the stadium." Needless to say, I stopped and watched the Tigers sting the Yellow Jackets.

Final Score: #12 Clemson 30 Georgia Tech 13

While working the 1989 ACC Baseball Tournament in Greenville, an NC State player decided that my tail looked like a play toy and started to pull on it. I put my hand out to shake hands but just as he reached for me, I grabbed his hat and took off. The crowd laughed loudly when they noticed that he was bald and embarrassed. Next thing I knew, I got a message that the NC State coach, Ray Tanner, was going to protest to the league office about my behavior. That coach is now the athletic director at the University of South Carolina.

Final Score: Clemson 9   NC State 2

During Halloween 1994, I was visiting my girlfriend, Suzanne Mullis, a College of Charleston graduate, in Charleston. Her roommate, who had introduced us, was CeCe Dalton. I was wearing one of the old Tiger suits as my costume. The girl standing next to me asked if she could hold the head. I said yes, and turned my back. The next thing I know, she disappeared. I didn't know her name, but all I could think was "Elvis has left the building." How often do you see a cougar come to the rescue of a Tiger? I didn't see Suzanne leave my side to chase after her. A couple of minutes later, she returned with my head in her hands. Since that day, she is still by my side, nothing has changed. We got married in 1995. Today, she keeps an eye on two Tigers, our son, Thomas, and myself.

STUART McWHORTER
#1 Tiger 1988-90
Bachelor of Science in Management '91
Master of Science in Health Administration '93
University of Alabama-Birmingham
Chairman
Clayton Associates
Residence - Nashville, Tenn.
Hometown - Atlanta, Ga.

During a rainy 1988 Clemson-Florida State game in Death Valley, I wet my tail and swung water, and maybe a little mud, towards the Florida State fans. They were next to The Hill, where Tiger Band sits today. After a couple of phone calls and letters, I had to go in front of the administration the next week to apologize. (This was the famous "Puntrooskie" game when a fake punt called by Seminoles Head Coach Bobby Bowden led to a game-winning touchdown.)

Final Score: #10 Florida State 24   #3 Clemson 21

While in the suit at a February 1989 basketball game, I approached ACC Official Lenny Wirtz during halftime to shake his hand. Without looking at me he said "Tiger boy, you'd better turn around and get away from me or I'll call a technical on you right now!" I did as instructed since

I didn't think Head Basketball Coach Cliff Ellis would have been too happy with me.

Final Score: Clemson 85   #8 North Carolina 82

Nine months later, we were staying at the hotel across the street from the Carolina Coliseum in Columbia. It didn't take long for someone to understand this rivalry. Our advisor had only been in Clemson for three years prior to this game. During those years, Clemson was 1-1-1 against South Carolina. He had the idea to display our 10'x15' Tiger Paw flag out the window. It took about 15 minutes and several complaints from South Carolina fans for the manager to knock on the door and order us to remove the flag.

At halftime, I went out on the field with a tuba to stir things up in the middle of the South Carolina band performance. Needless to say, I upset a lot of Gamecock fans and band members. But it was fun playing in a large polka band. Wish Lawrence Welk still had his big band television show.

Final Score: #15 Clemson 45   South Carolina 0

When making off-campus appearances, I was always amazed at how many women hosts would ask to help zip up the suit. Was it because of the man in the suit or the suit itself? Funny, they were not around when it was time to get out. During these appearances, the older kids would pull the tail and poke their fingers in the holes of the eyes. I couldn't talk, so a good firm handshake usually would solve the problem.

All the mascots who have worked the Sun Fun Festival in Myrtle Beach will agree it is one of the best events in the state. I don't know if it is the sun, the beach, or the ladies on the Tropicana Suntan Lotion float.

If you want to visit a patriotic city, then Easley and its 4th of July parade is a good place to start. Especially if you like to dance to the Carolina shag while riding on a float in a parade. I will never forget Ace Bowie coming to my rescue from the ladies during one of the hottest days of the years. Ace used to sing in a beach band, Pieces of 8, with former Head Basketball Coach Cliff Ellis as a guest singer on several occasions.

Easley is the hometown of Army Captain Kimberley Nicole Hampton, the first woman combat pilot to be killed in battle. If you are driving on Highway 88 near the community called Slabtown, there is a stretch of the road, along with the Pickens County Public Library in Easley, named in her honor. Her mother, Ann Hampton, wrote a book about her life titled "Kimberly's Flight."

A common denominator shared among all the mascots or any Clemson student is that we all want to give back. The thousands of hours we have all been in the suit whether at an athletic event, a parade, or visiting someone in a hospital is a great way to give back.

In the mid-1990s, George Bennett, then the executive director of IP-TAY, approached my family about making a donation for a statue of The Tiger to be placed next to Memorial Stadium. The original idea was for two giant Tigers, similar to the one that guards Littlejohn Coliseum. As time passed, a decision was made for a more playful Tiger to reflect the one that roams along the sideline.

Today, The Tiger stands at Gate 1 of Memorial Stadium, pointing to the sky, just like many coaches and players do prior to running down The Hill. The statue's location is symbolic since it is next to gate one where the students enter the stadium.

CHAPTER FIVE
THE 1990s

WILL SYKES
No. 1 Tiger 1990-92
Bachelor of Science in Mechanical Engineering '92
Millwork Sales and Manufacturing
VictorBilt, Inc.
Residence and Hometown - Greenville, S.C.

The 1990 appearance at the East Region of the NCAA basketball tournament stands as the top of my experiences in the suit. The tournament kept me from having spring break in Florida. Instead, I was on a plane headed to Hartford, Conn. along with the ACC regular season champion Clemson Tigers to face the

Brigham Young University Cougars. Back then, only The Tiger went to the post-season games. There was no pep band or cheerleaders because being known as a football school, most students always had plans to head south for spring break. It was just me and several hundred Clemson fans in the 20,000-seat arena. Almost! The Athletic Department hired the Central Connecticut State University pep band for $2,000. Everyone in the

band got an orange Clemson shirt and face paint. It was a wise financial decision that the department made for several years, until the NCAA appropriated enough money for the institutions to take a mascot, 12 cheerleaders/dancers and 30 band members to each round of the tournament.

Final Score: #17 Clemson 49   BYU 47

Maybe Hartford wasn't so bad. Two days later, during the second round, the Tigers played the LaSalle Explorers from Philadelphia, a member of the Atlantic 10 Conference. La Salle had previously won the NCAA basketball championship way back in 1954. (They used to play their home games in The Palestra, with Pennsylvania, Saint Joseph's, Temple, and Villanova.) After trailing by 19, the Tigers came back to beat the Explorers. The Clemson Lady Tigers once played UCONN in the Elite Eight of the NCAA tournament in The Palestra.

Final Score: #17 Clemson 79 #12 La Salle 75

Two games, two wins and now on to the Sweet 16 to play the Connecticut Huskies. It's the back end of spring break. I'm thinking at this point, who needs Florida, when the winner of this game plays Duke or UCLA in the Elite Eight? The next game was in East Rutherford, N.J. at the Brendan Byrne Arena. The arena is named after the 47th governor of New Jersey, who had a daughter graduate from Clemson. The partisan crowd that filled the arena that night was pulling against us. Everyone wanted UCONN to play Duke or UCLA. The Clemson Pep Band was in attendance the second weekend holding up a sign to the CBS cameras that stated they were the real Clemson band.

The overall experience now in our third game was pure joy. However, everything would change in a blink of an eye, at the end of the third round game against UCONN. The Huskies' Tate George killed our massive 19-point comeback and stole the game-winning shot status from David Young (my Greenville high school teammate) who had just made a three-pointer to take the lead with 1.6 seconds to play. It went from the highest Clemson basketball moment I had ever experienced to the lowest in just under two seconds. Two days later, Christian Laettner hit a turnaround jump shot to send Duke, whom we had beaten two weeks earlier at Clemson, to the Final Four. I still don't see how Laettner's shot is better than Tate George's on-the-run over the extended arms of Sean Tyson that sent the Tigers home.

Final Score: #3 UCONN 71 #17 Clemson 70

Five and a half months later, it's football season when the Tigers kick off against the Long Beach State 49ers. It's the toughest environment for any mascot to make it through for several reasons. It's the first game of the year, kickoff is at the traditional one o'clock start and it's 90 degrees. There is no way you can prepare for the first game, unless you get in the suit and do pushups on the ground several weeks prior to the game in the middle of the afternoon.

I started the day off with the pregame parade, followed by four quarters of a football game, and after 303 pushups, I was totally exhausted. I lost between 10 and 12 pounds and got ridiculed because of my lousy pushups late in the game. If you sat in the stands throughout the entire game, you might be able to visualize what it was like to be in the suit doing all those pushups. The end result was a Clemson win; however, there would be some sad news concerning the 49er program three months later. Their 72-year-old Head Coach George Allen would pass away on New Year's Eve. Yes, George Allen, the NFL Hall of Fame coach who led the Washington Redskins to the 1972 NFC championship. After one more season, Long Beach State would stop funding their football program.

Final Score: #10 Clemson 59   Long Beach State 0

It's always good to wear a tuxedo to Homecoming. At halftime, I got to ride on the SAE float with the 1990 Queen and Court. Our queen was Stephanie Bowie, a varsity cheerleader from Easley. I guess I was Stephanie's knight in an orange furry suit instead of shining armor. However, this knight lost his queen to a king named Todd, who became Stephanie's husband in 1992.

Final Score: #19 Clemson 26   Duke 7

The Tigers were invited to play Duke in the Tokyo Dome the next year. The game was called the Coca-Cola Classic. It was the first time the Tigers had played in Tokyo since 1982, when they defeated Wake Forest, 21-17. That game was called the Mirage Bowl.

The week in Tokyo had seen numerous joint appearances with the Clemson and Duke players, cheerleaders and band. In the second half of the game, the Duke band called me over for a photo, so I obliged. As I was walking back onto the field, the suit felt odd 'til I figured out someone from the Duke band had cut my tail off. I was embarrassed. Without the tail, I failed to do my last set of pushups, costing me a record for the most pushups at an overseas game. The new record would have been 101.

The Tigers won the game and the ACC Championship, which meant a trip to the Citrus Bowl in Orlando, Fla. to play the University of California. The sign I was holding up proclaiming Clemson's championship got in the newspaper the next day and then on the wall at Mac's Drive In, the famous restaurant between Clemson and Pendleton.

Final Score: #13 Clemson 31 Duke 21

Operation Desert Storm was the name given to the First Gulf War on January 16, 1991. That evening the basketball Tigers defeated Western Carolina 103-82.

Three days later, we were hosting Temple when those in attendance were given patriotic ribbons as they entered Littlejohn Coliseum. The Rally

Cats, cheerleaders, and The Tiger wore a t-shirt that said, "Til They Come Home, Wear A Ribbon." It was also the day that Go, the mascot of the NBA Phoenix Suns, was in town to entertain the crowd. During the game, Go, a guerilla, was handed an American flag after he had jumped up on the basketball rim bringing the crowd to their feet in honor of the brave men and women in our Armed Forces who were entering the field of battle.

Two of the most famous residences in Clemson in the 1980s were the home of the president of Clemson University and Coach Danny Ford's home. Other than players or coaches, I doubt if many people had ever been invited to Coach Ford's house. The house (part of his contract) was given to him to live in by the Athletic Department for winning the 1981 National Championship.

A trivia question that legendary Sports Information Director Tim Bourret could not answer if asked would be, "Who lived in Coach Ford's house after his coaching tenure at Clemson?" Answer: My roommate Will McCauley and I until the house was sold. How fitting for a mascot. It has a giant Tiger Paw on the bottom of the backyard pool.

CHRIS PETERS

No. 1 Tiger 1992-93
Bachelor of Science in Financial Management '91
Master of Business Administration '93
Senior Director of Development
Clemson University Foundation
Residence - Charlotte, N.C.
Hometown - Walkersville, Md.

Watching the first football game my freshman year in 1989 from The Hill, I was enamored with The Tiger along with a female cheerleader named Leslie Yoakum. A couple of weeks later, I became a member of Central Spirit and the Student Alumni Council. My sophomore year, I pledged the Pi Kappa Alpha fraternity and got to meet the '86 Tiger, Chris Shimakonis. At 19, it was cool to join a fraternity that had a tradition of having brothers who had been on the cheerleading squad and served as The Tiger. These included mic man Brian Aiken and cheerleaders Woody Binnicker, Joe Erwin, Gordy Farr, and Brian Garrison, to name a few.

Becoming The Tiger can be a journey. My journey started with me firing the cannon. When I took the field at the University of Georgia in 1991, after specifically being told not to bring the cannon, it was promptly confiscated by representatives of Georgia's law enforcement community.

Final Score: Georgia 27 #6 Clemson 12

In 1991, Head Football Coach Ken Hatfield brought back the color purple into the football jerseys and across the Clemson landscape. Purple had been one of the original school colors. One of the coolest things to happen to me as The Tiger was when running back Rudy Harris picked me up over his head after he scored a touchdown on a three-yard run against NC State. This was one of the first times the team wore the new purple jerseys. It surprised me because I was 6'1" and 200 pounds. Strength Coach Gary Wade and his staff had the team in great shape.

Final Score: #19 Clemson 29 #12 NC State 19

If you are in charge of firing the cannon, they throw you a bone and you get to be the backup Tiger, if needed, for an event. One of my funniest stories happened on a day when I was in the suit riding a moped in front

To my good friend,
Christopher M. Peters, with
best wishes -
Strom Thurmond

of the President's House. I was pulled over by a representative of the Clemson University law enforcement community. An officer from the second car that arrived on the scene chastised the young officer for pulling me over. The first officer's question to me when he walked up was, "Can you see in that thing?" It is still funny today, but not a wise move, especially for you youngsters riding a moped. I am thankful that I never had to call South Carolina's senior statesman in the U.S. Senate, The Honorable Senator Strom Thurmond.

In the spring of 1992, my journey was moving forward as I decided once again I wanted to be The Tiger. I was practicing my skit in a small patch of grass behind the Dillard Building the morning of tryouts. Once again, a representative of the Clemson University law enforcement community in a cruiser stopped, and an officer got out and questioned me. He thought I was drunk after having watched me do a pantomime skit of a day at the beach (surfing, girl watching, sun tanning, and being attacked by a shark). At the time, I didn't know if this was a good or bad sign. Ten hours later, I was filled with enormous pride and reverence for being allowed to serve Clemson in this prestigious manner, while carrying on the tradition of a PiKA as The Tiger.

The Tigers began the 1992 football season as the defending ACC champions. My first game in the suit as the No. 1 mascot was against Ball State University. All anyone wanted to know that weekend was whether or not David Lettermen, a Ball State alumnus, was at the game. One thing for sure is we never made Dave's "Top 10" list the Monday after the game.

Final Score: #13 Clemson 24   Ball State 10

A week later, everyone got ready for Florida State, the newest member of the ACC, to make their first appearance in Death Valley since 1988. It was also the first night game since 1956 at Clemson, and a pep rally was being held in the amphitheater. There was a traditional orange Clemson sunset as I lighted my spear to make fun of the FSU mascot Chief Osceola, who usually entered their home games on a horse named Renegade. After a couple of minutes, I tried to stomp out the fire, nearly catching my Tiger suit on fire. It was a little tougher than I thought; however, I successfully extinguished the fire. Unfortunately, the Seminoles were on fire the next day since they came back to beat us in the fourth quarter.

Final Score: #5 Florida State 24   #15 Clemson 20

A picture of the comeback against Virginia hangs under the north and south stands of Memorial Stadium. Down 28-0, the Tigers scored the last 29 points, including a last-minute field goal by Nelson Welch. A great mid-afternoon day to be in the suit.

Final Score: #25 Clemson 29   #10 Virginia 28

The next week, still riding a high from the Virginia game, the Blue Devil mascot was in my way when I came down The Hill through Tiger Band. After some tousling, I stole his pitchfork and sprinted from the west end zone all the way back to our student section where I proceeded to humiliate him to the joy of our students. I could give more details, but let's just say I hit him so hard in the head with my tail that I could see 50 percent of his real face.

Final Score: #19 Clemson 21   Duke 6

Whether it was being at the Egg Scramble Jamboree, at one of the
Barnyard Burn pep rallies (1988, 1990, 1992, and 1994) prior to the South Carolina game, or in a parade at Disney World with Tigger and Mickey Mouse before the New Year's Day Citrus Bowl in 1992, each mascot's journey is unique.

The kids we entertain make all the sweat worth every minute in the suit. Our rewards range from being in a Toys for Tots commercial with Cocky and the U.S. Marines to attending a festival in Myrtle Beach with girls from Hooters of America. (Hooters was owned at the time by 1960 Clemson alumnus Bob Brooks, whose name is on the Brooks Center for the Performing Arts.)

Looking back at my journey, it's amazing all the people I met and became friends with outside of the suit. The year after I graduated, I was talking to The Tiger in Chapel Hill. A little boy named Christopher was there watching The Tiger, just like all the Clemson fans do when attending a game. I offered to take his picture and send it to his mom Sally Robbins Summerlin, who had played tennis at Clemson (1976-80), and his dad Bruce, who was the human relations director at Shorewood Packaging in LaGrange, Ga. That picture led to an interview with Bruce, who then hired me for a sales position. Just think, it all started because I took a child's photo with The Tiger. Years later, Christopher would become Smokey, the student mascot at the University of Tennessee. I'm glad he became a mascot, but he chose the wrong color of orange.

Being The Tiger is the highest and most unique honor at Clemson. It is right there with getting your class ring and being tapped for Tiger Brotherhood, an honorary fraternity started in 1928.

And yes, I really did smile in every photo I took, just like The Tiger did in Chapel Hill.

CHASE NICHOLS
No. 1 Tiger 1993-94
Bachelor of Science in Marketing '94
Director of Marketing
AssessMD
Residence - McKinney, TX
Hometown - Kingsport, TN

After being a cheerleader for three years, I thought it would be an amazing experience to see Clemson through the eyes of The Tiger. During my interview, I was asked if I was selected, would I tell everyone (even classmates) that I was The Tiger. I said no, because I think it removes some of the magic out of getting to see and interact with The Tiger, especially if you have an image of who is in the suit.

As a cheerleader, you have the opportunity to stand on the field holding and waving the giant Clemson flag as the buses deliver the team to the top of The Hill just before the beginning of the game.

As The Tiger, you are in the middle of the action stationed high on The Hill,

feeling the excitement and energy of the crowd as you say a short prayer–a prayer that you don't trip after the cannon fires and you're sprinting down The Hill with 120 players and coaches gaining speed behind you. It's an amazing rush!

No matter the score of any game, as a cheerleader or a mascot, it is our job to remain upbeat and energetic. While in The Tiger suit in Tallahassee, Fla., I saw former Dallas Cowboys Hall of Fame running back Emmitt Smith sitting on the Clemson bench watching his brother, Emory, a running back, play for Clemson.

So I strutted over to our bench and chatted with the Cowboy legend. I told Emmitt we could really use him in our backfield right now and asked if he wouldn't mind suiting up. He laughed. One of the photographers took a photo of that moment. My sister, Morri ('92), later framed that picture for me. I still have it today.

Final Score: #1 Florida State 57   #21 Clemson 0

Staying upbeat, the Tigers went 6-2 in the next eight games heading to the season finale in Columbia. It doesn't matter when, where, or which athletic team is playing South Carolina. There can be nothing finer than beating Carolina.

Final Score: #24 Clemson 16   South Carolina 13

MIKE BAYS
No. 1 Tiger 1994-97
Bachelor of Science in Management '97
Master of Human Resource Development '99
Professional Recruiter
Godshall Staffing
Residence - Easley, S.C.
Hometown - Bethlehem, Pa.

The 655 miles from Bethlehem, Pa. to Columbia, S.C. is how I started my trip to someday be The Tiger. My rejection letter from the admissions office at Clemson stated that if I kept my grades up I could transfer in from the University of South Carolina. It wasn't until I graduated that I approached Randy Boatwright, who now works in the CU Alumni Association, and told him that his letter in 1992 originally sent this Tiger to

Columbia instead of Clemson.

Florida State's football program was involved in a little shoe scandal after winning the 1993 National Championship. Eight players had shopped at a Foot Locker store in which they received approximately $6,000 in shoes paid for by an unregistered agent. Rival football Coach Steve Spurrier, who was at the University of Florida at the time, said in an interview that FSU meant "Free Shoes University."

It was common to throw t-shirts into the crowd at basketball games. Prior to our February 19, 1994 contest against Florida State, I went to a Foot Locker and collected some bags. During a time out, I pranced onto the floor with a "FSU – Free Shoes University" sign. A second timeout and another sign, this one reading, "Tomahawk Shop," with a basketball shoe dangling from the end of the stick. Finally, with my Foot Locker bags in hand, instead of tossing t-shirts, I began to toss empty shoe boxes that I had gotten from the equipment room into the crowd. How ironic, the game was decided by a spread equal to the number of players involved in the scandal. Later that evening I got a call from the principal's office, aka the administration. These harmless pranks, though unsportsmanlike, are what makes one mascot different from another.

Final Score: Florida State 79 Clemson 71

The summer of 1994 coincided with my sister's wedding back home. The suit was sent FedEx to me for a surprise appearance from the Clemson Ti-

ger. I slipped out of my tux and into the suit and planned with the disc jockey to play a song dedicated to the bride from her brother, The Tiger. Little did I know that "Sea of Love" by the Honeydrippers was my new brother-in-law's choice for a wedding song with his new bride. The announcement was made and here came The Tiger! The song cued up? You guessed it – "Tiger Rag."

With the wedding behind me, it was time to get back to campus for the Welcome Back Festival followed by the

First Friday Parade. The Tigers had a rough year on the football field that season, so let's move forward to the 1994-95 basketball season and welcome Head Coach Rick Barnes to Tigertown.

The Duke men's basketball team, usually led by Head Coach Mike Krzyzewski, who did not make the trip due to a severe back problem, visited Littlejohn Coliseum on Feb. 4, 1995. The shoe was now on the other foot. The Blue Devils were in last place in the ACC. During a timeout, I walked around the court handing out donuts. The donuts represented the number of conference wins Duke had up to this point in the season. With my tray of donuts and a sign that read "Duke's ACC Wins: Powdered or Glazed," I approached the section behind the Duke bench where it is mandated by the ACC to hold 75 seats for the visiting team. Suddenly, wham, the mom of Duke's starting point guard Steve Wojciechowski knocked the tray of donuts out of my hands. The crowd went nuts. I dropped my head, with my shoulders slouched, as I walked off the floor. The winless streak continued as Rick Barnes's "Slab Five" swept the Blue Devils.

Final Score: Clemson 51 Duke 44

The year was 1995, and in honor of the 100th anniversary of Clemson Football, the Tigers wore throwback uniforms and helmets for a 6:39 p.m. kickoff against the Georgia Bulldogs. The unique kickoff time honored the Tigers' 6-3 victory in the Cotton Bowl against Boston College to end the 1939 season. It would become Clemson's first of many bowl games.

We did not have music pumped in back then, so when I raised my hand, the crowd got louder. The suit was magic; unfortunately the throwback uniforms were not. The only other time we wore the uniforms was for the opening game against Furman in 1996.

Final Score: Georgia 19 Clemson 17

You always see Clark Kent run into a phone booth to change into his Superman costume, but you never could see where he left his clothes. As mascots, we changed in the strangest places. I was friends with Mack Ammick, who played Cocky in 1995. Mack had me change in one of the offices under the home stands at Williams-Brice Stadium.

The rivalry always had at least one play that would live in your mind forever. On this Saturday afternoon, it was Clemson's Emory Smith rambling down the field carrying a South Carolina defender for 20 yards before finally being dragged out of bounds at the 7-yard line after a 54-yard gain. It was at this moment, with less than nine minutes to go in the fourth quarter, that everyone in attendance knew the game was over. After celebrating the win on the field, it was time to change out of my Tiger suit.

What Mack failed to tell me was my exit was through the post-game South Carolina interview area. I heard people yelling at me to get out of there, thinking that I was going under the stadium to rub in the win. After quickly getting to the office, I changed into Clark Kent, threw my suit in the bag and made it safely out of the Hen House. I can't imagine what might have happened if the role had been reversed.

Final Score: #24 Clemson 38   South Carolina 17

The Tiger and Cocky make appearances all over the state of South Carolina. My favorite joint appearance was in Laurens for former Tiger mascot Martin Lowry. Although rivals, Cocky and I were friends and trusted each other. On this evening, we decided to change suits. Everyone who always loved me disliked me on this night and vice versa.

You always see people hold up signs saying "HI MOM." All Tiger mascots, whether male or female, have a dad. Tigerama 1996 celebrated "A Rock Solid Tradition for 100 Years" of Clemson Football. On this evening, my dad, Gary, was in attendance, dressed in an old Tiger suit, but he added a long white beard, sports coat, a hat and a walking cane with a horn. We danced around the coliseum to "Tiger Rag." Thanks, Dad, for this special moment. It was like when Ken Griffey, Sr. and Ken Griffey, Jr. played in a game for the Seattle Mariners on August 31, 1990 against the Kansas City Royals.

Prior to the 1996 Peach Bowl, I made a trip to my hometown in Pennsylvania. I asked my friend Eric Schultz, who was home from the University of Pittsburgh, if he had plans for New Year's. I told him if he didn't, to come with me to Atlanta for the Peach Bowl. On game day, with me carrying The Tiger suit in a bag and Eric wearing my sideline pass, we entered the Georgia Dome. One of my childhood friends got the best view in the house. In 1997, the bowl name would be changed to the Chick-fil-A Peach Bowl.

Final Score: #17 LSU 10 Clemson 7

"Fool me once, shame on you: fool me twice, shame on me." While finishing my master's degree in 1999, it was time again to see if I could get another friend, this time Phil Sienkowski, into a game in Atlanta. This time it was prior to playing Georgia Tech. Everything worked according to our plan as we entered the field on the Tech sideline, made our introductions, and headed over to the Clemson sideline to do some stretching. Every time Clemson scored, I ran the Tiger Paw flag through the end zone. We had fooled the guards not once, but twice; however, we lost both games.

Final Score: #13 Georgia Tech 45 Clemson 42

Once a Tiger, whether a student, an alum, a fan or The Tiger, you will always be a Tiger. In 2003, the then-Tiger Brad Stoehr needed a replacement for the Georgia Tech game in Atlanta. It had been six years since I was the full-time mascot. It's that once-in-a-lifetime chance to relive those "Glory Days" that made Bruce Springsteen a legend. I got to go "Back to the Future" (referring to the movie and its sequels by another Michael, Michael J. Fox). I found out later that Brad went to a Dave Matthews concert.

Final Score: Clemson 39 Georgia Tech 3

In 2010, at the age of 36, I became the Brett Favre of Clemson mascots when once again I put on the suit. This time, it was at a home basketball game with my four-year-old son Lance in attendance and prior to my second, son, Jake, being born in 2011. Maybe there is one more appearance left in me. Probably I should do it when Brett goes into the Packer or NFL Hall of Fame, since I am the all-time pushup record holder with 2,216.

WES SCRUGGS
No. 1 Tiger 1997-98
Bachelor of Science in Financial Management '99
Master of Business Administration '04
UNC-Charlotte
Director of Performance Groups Premier, Inc.
Residence - Charlotte, N.C.
Hometown - Gaffney, S.C.

As a wide-eyed freshman in 1995, full of energy and expectations, I got my first taste of what being a Clemson Tiger meant. It was the first time I realized The Tiger was more than a figure at sporting events. He represented the university at all events and was an ambassador to drive school spirit and recognition. At that first encounter, I walked up to Mike Bays, who was in the suit, and asked, "How can I do that?"

Everyone dreams about playing college or pro sports. My wildest dream was walking onto the basketball team. In high school, I was the starting center, so I was thinking maybe I could play in the low post. With my 6'2" frame, reality hit me when two new freshman centers, Tom Wideman (6'10") and Harold "Big O" Jamison (6'8") came walking out of the locker room. Mascot tryouts, here I come. After all, I had played the Indian at Gaffney High School.

After the mascot tryouts, I still wasn't the No. 1 mascot. As the backup, I spent all my time working women's soccer and basketball games and various other appearances.

After a solid year as the backup, I went into the next tryouts with a distinct advantage, but not with the expectation of being chosen The Tiger. The trip back to Jervey later that evening to see the results seemed to take much longer than usual, and the anticipation of discovering the outcome had me a little worked up. The excitement of seeing my name as The Tiger for the first time was pretty cool. I couldn't wait to tell my roommates, family, and friends. My first official appearance as The Tiger was at a baseball game. I was so nervous, I don't remember the game, but I do know I cherished every moment.

As fall of my junior year rolled in, I was floating with the knowledge that I would not only be rubbing Howard's Rock and leading the Tigers onto the field, but I would also be representing the university. The pride of being the literal face of Clemson University was astounding.

The most memorable part of the football season for me was the season-long wrestling skits with Ryan Teten, the Tiger Cub. Both of us loved to watch professional wrestling which was extremely popular at the time. World Championship Wrestling produced a show called "Monday Night Nitro."

At that first game, we came out of our dressing room wearing our "nWo" shirts. The wrestling fans–mainly adult males and young boys–went nuts. We wore a different wrestling shirt each game. If the other team had a mascot, Ryan and I would wear shirts of wrestlers that were teamed together on television and attack the visiting mascot. If there wasn't a visiting mascot, we would wear opposing shirts and attack each other. It never failed to get a huge rise out of the fans.

It was Military Appreciation Day when Duke came to Death Valley. The Blue Devil said he was sick and did not want to mess around. In true wrestling fashion, the Devil attacked the Cub from behind in the second quarter, obviously feeling much better.

After halftime, we put our wrestling shirts on and went to work. It was war. We pounced on the Devil when he accidently walked too close to our student section. Once on the ground, we proceeded to execute multiple wrestling moves such as leg drops, elbow drops, body flops and a flying frog splash, an Eddie Guerrero move.

A student worker, Dana Marangelli, sent a clip of our skits to World Championship Wrestling in Atlanta. WCW was having "Monday Night Nitro" parties around the country. Before you knew it, WCW was in Death Valley. Students and local wrestling fans were invited to the live viewing party on the video board in the west end zone.

Mike Bays wore a Lucha Libre mask and served as emcee. WCW sent "Hacksaw" Jim Dugan, "Disco Inferno" and a few of the "Nitro Girls" to participate in the festivities. One was Kimberley, the wife of "Diamond" Dallas Page.

Final Score: Clemson 29 Duke 20

ESPN was getting in the commercial business to promote their network. They were using professional athletes and mascots in their skits and invited me to Bristol, Conn. to be in a commercial. On that trip, I had breakfast with ESPN personality Dan Patrick (although this is Mark Jones in the picture). He was genuinely interested in me as a person and shared stories

about his family. I met the greatest mascot of all time, Ted Giannoulas, the San Diego Chicken; Morganna Roberts, the Kissing Bandit; tennis star Pete Sampras; and Big Al, the University of Alabama mascot. Unfortunately, Big Al and I ended up on the cutting room floor.

I was in the ESPN commercial commemorating Dan Patrick's 2,000th "SportsCenter" show. Morganna rode in on a lawnmower as his gift. The same day I was cut, the San Diego Chicken was wreaking havoc all over the set, and at the end of the commercial, they got his head off and it was tennis pro Sampras dressed as the Chicken.

The biggest celebrities Clemson had at the time were Head Football Coach Tommy West and Head Basketball Coach Rick Barnes. I got to travel with them to IPTAY events. Off-camera they were funny, sharing stories. As big as they were, once someone found out I was The Tiger, the focus shifted to me. Fans want to know what the experience is like in the suit. Thank you, fans, for your attention; it is very much appreciated by all the mascots.

In February 2015, the athletic department needed a mascot for the Farmers Insurance Open, which is one of the first tournaments on the PGA Tour. I was going to be in California so I volunteered for the event. Next thing you know I'm in a room with the Stanford Tree, the Oregon Duck, the Florida Gator Albert, Pistol Pete from Oklahoma State, St. John's Johnny Thunderbird, and the University of San Diego's mascot Diego Torero.

It was a fun event, meeting my counterparts. However, at the end of the day, standing at the 18th hole next to former Clemson golfer and the 2009 U.S. Open Champion Lucas Glover (right), was the highlight for this Tiger.

ROB LOCKARD
No. 1 Tiger 1998-99
Bachelor of Science in Secondary Education '99
Master of Human Resource Development '01
Human Resource Manager
Residence - Kansas City, Mo.
Hometown - Lexington Park, Md.

The 1998 student mascot for the University of North Carolina played an awesome trick on me when we visited Chapel Hill, N.C. for a football game. UNC's mascot is named Rameses. Rameses thought it would be a good idea for us to get down in a three-point stance and clothesline a couple of North Carolina state troopers who were sitting on a nearby low concrete wall. I figured that they had seen us and would play along. Rameses shouted, "One, two, three" and I took off, plowing over one of the troopers. When I got up and looked around, there was Rameses pointing and laughing at me. It seems he never hit his officer. The officer I tackled got up, dusted himself off, looked at a group of his fellow policemen (who were now laughing) and then looked back at me. He then grabbed me by the arm, leaned in, and said, "You are lucky you are in that suit."

Final Score: North Carolina 21 Clemson 14

The goal is to always make it through to the NCAA "Final Four" tournament in basketball. The consolation if not selected to the big dance is the National Invitation Tournament. In 1999, The Tigers advanced to the NIT finals in New York City instead of the NCAA finals in St. Petersburg, Fla.

Here is my week-long experience. We stayed at the Marriott Marquis in Times Square, just a few blocks from Madison Square Garden where the games were being played. The University of Oregon was also in the four-team tournament. Their mascot, The Duck, introduced me to Ahmad Rashad, an Oregon alum, and a Minnesota Viking four-time Pro Bowl selection. Towards the end of the week, the main security guard to the basketball court started treating me like royalty, saying, "Yes, Mr. Tiger. Whatever you need, Mr. Tiger," as I approached the court from the dressing room tunnel. I felt like the mayor of the city.

During the trip we went to "The Today Show." While in the suit, I got to do the weather with Al Roker. During the show I scored a kiss on the nose from the legendary television anchorwoman Jane Pauley.

In the city, you can do and see just about everything. They say the NYPD is the finest. Yes, they are, especially when an officer on horseback in Central Park trades you his hat for a couple of Clemson t-shirts. However, the absolute best part of the trip was getting a cab ride from a Clemson graduate. When he opened the trunk of his car, it was a museum of Clemson paraphernalia. It's unfortunate that Clemson Hall of Fame Broadcaster Jim Phillips has passed away. Mr. Phillips would be able to tell you who the cabbie is for your next trip to the Big Apple. They were best friends.

Final Score: Clemson 79   Xavier 76
California 61   Clemson 60

ZACK CALLAHAM

No. 1 Tiger 1999-00
Bachelor of Science in Marketing '00
Customer Support E-Commerce
Super Duper Publications
Residence - Powdersville, S.C.
Hometown - Belton, S.C.

In 1998 I was disappointed after not being selected to be The Tiger. My tryout consisted of a skit about Head Basketball Coach Rick Barnes abandoning ship for Texas a month earlier. Looking back, my skit was too long and boring in front of the judges. Mascots are supposed to be concise in their skits and antics.

You learn from your mistakes, so in 1999 I shortened my skit and was selected. What a year to be in the suit!

My inaugural game was also the first for new Head Football Coach Tommy Bowden. Coach Bowden had joined Clemson after going 12-0 the year before at Tulane University. Our first opponent was Marshall University. Tragedy had struck this school in 1970, when Marshall lost 37 players, 8 coaches and 25 boosters along with 5 crew members in a Southern Airways plane crash. (A movie about the crash called "We Are Marshall" premiered in 2006 with Matthew McConaughey as Head Coach Jack Lengyel.)

Like my first attempt to be the mascot, Coach Bowden lost his first game as the Tigers head coach. Marshall went on to an undefeated 13-0 season and Coach Bowden finished the season 6-6 overall and 5-3 in the ACC to win his first ACC Coach of the Year award. The nighttime atmosphere and having the son of legendary Coach Bobby Bowden as our new coach was breathtaking for this rookie mascot.

Final Score: #10 Marshall 13   Clemson 10

Halfway through the season, the Tigers were 3-3 heading into the biggest media frenzy game in Memorial Stadium history with Bowden Bowl I. The night prior to the game, Midnight Madness took place in Littlejohn Coliseum. Twenty-four hours later, I was being instructed to get out of the suit. What led to my discipline all started that Friday night, when I was in the tunnel of the coliseum talking to two former mascots, Martin Lowry and Stuart McWhorter.

They challenged the Cub and me to make fun of Peter Warrick the next day. Warrick was the Florida State wide receiver who started the season as the front runner for the Heisman Trophy. Unfortunately, on September 29, Warrick and two others were arrested on grand theft charges for purchasing $412.38 worth of clothing for only $21.40 from a Dillard's department store in Tallahassee, Fla. Warrick would later plead guilty to misdemeanor petty theft and serve a two-game suspension from the football team.

Prior to the football game, the Athletic Department had asked all the in-house cameramen not to show any signs in the stands about Warrick's situation. As the game progressed, the Cub and I slipped on a pair of criminal overalls to mock Warrick. We started at the student section and walked behind our bench and then in front of the FSU band in the west end zone. It was at this time that one of the in-house cameramen spotted us and the director put us up on Pawvision, the video board over The Hill. We were quickly removed from the field.

In reviewing the case after the game, the cameraman didn't see a problem showing the mascots, since they were a part of the Athletic Department and not a sign in the stadium. The mascot advisor was unaware of the stunt. However, he had warned us not to make fun of Warrick. So you are 20 years old, and it is your job to entertain. You are challenged the night prior by former mascots. What are you supposed to do, ask for permission or forgiveness? We didn't get suspended like Warrick did. However, we did have to meet with the administration and apologize.

Final Score: #1 Florida State 17   Clemson 14

Being The Tiger was the ultimate way to be yourself, especially when they give you a lanyard and a pass that reads: "EVERYWHERE." Not until I think back on that pass do I see the symbolism. It wasn't where The Tiger was allowed, but where he already was. Corny, I know, but so true.

CHAPTER SIX
THE 2000s

JON POTTER
No. 1 Tiger 2000-01
Bachelor of Science in Ceramic Engineering '01
Master of Business Administration '11
University of South Carolina
Product Manager
AFL
Residence - Reidville, S.C.
Hometown - Anderson, S.C.

It's amazing how you can be in the right or wrong place during any game! On this occasion, the Cub and I were right in the middle of all the action. We were playing the Seminoles in Bowden Bowl II in Tallahassee, Fla. My roommate, Jamie Somaini, punted and pinned the 'Noles on their 1-yard line. Chris Weinke pulled the best play-action fake I've ever seen and the best since "Puntrooskie." The entire stadium thought the running back was stonewalled at the line of scrimmage, as Weinke was selling the fake with his back turned to the line of scrimmage. There we were under the goal post as we saw the ball in Weinke's gut the entire time. He spun around and threw a 99-yard touchdown pass to receiver "Snoop" Minnis. You don't win a national championship (1999) or the Heisman Trophy (2000) without luck and trick plays. FSU and Weinke did both.

Final Score: #4 Florida State 54   #10 Clemson 7

There are two absolutely unforgettable catches in Clemson Football history. The first catch was on November 19, 1977, when Clemson Hall of Fame wide receiver Jerry Butler made a falling backwards 20-yard catch for a touchdown. The pass from future Clemson Ring of Honor quarterback Steve Fuller to Butler gave the 15th ranked Tigers a 31-27 win over the Gamecocks in Columbia, with just 49 seconds left in the game.

The second catch took place almost 23 years later to the day on November 18, 2000. I was standing on the mic man platform on the southeast 10-yard line of Memorial Stadium. South Carolina was up 14-13 with 10 seconds to play. The Gamecock offensive coaches had already taken the elevators down to the field to celebrate what would have been their 36th win in the 98th game of the series. Clemson had the ball on their own 42-yard line when quarterback Woody Dantzler threw a 50-yard pass to the falling out-of-bounds wide receiver, Rod Garner, at the 8-yard line. Gardner's catch, in front of the second largest crowd (85,187) in this historic series, set up Clemson's 25-yard game winning field goal by Aaron Hunt for their 59th win in a series that began in 1896. Those watching the game on a large screen outside the Esso Club said the crowd's roar sounded like a jet taking off when Gardner made the second catch.

Final Score: #16 Clemson 16   #25 South Carolina 14

Prior to the 2001 Gator Bowl, I had heard the pre-game parade progressed around the city of Jacksonville, Fla. There is no way you can walk three-plus miles and then work a three-hour football game. It was my lucky day when the The Paw Bearer (a 1967 Cadillac hearse) being driven by Jeff Herbert came by where the cheerleaders and I were standing. (The Herbert family owns the Boscobel Golf and Country Club in Pendleton.) I jumped on the hood of the moving hearse as the parade was going up a hill. While executing this move, my tail got caught under the wheel and

ripped off. I picked it up and the cheerleaders handed me a roll of athletic tape. Then, I jumped inside the car where Jim Southerlin made some quick repairs. After the parade, a sponsor for Tiger Band had a sewing kit, thus saving me from the wrath of the former mascots. The hearse has been parked along Centennial Boulevard since 1981. Stop by for a picture.

Final Score: #6 Virginia Tech 41   #16 Clemson 20

The Carolina Panthers Top Cats performed in Littlejohn Coliseum at halftime of the NC State game in 2001. Saturdays in January were and still are on-campus recruiting days for football. The Top Cats walked by recruits and their parents in the tunnel of the coliseum. Don't know who

the recruits were that day; however, here are some of the players who signed a letter of intent a month later: Roscoe Crosby, Maurice Fountain, Derrick Hamilton, Leroy Hill and two-sport athlete Airese Currie (football and track).

Final Score: Clemson 72 NC State 69

PATRICK HITPAS
No. 1 Tiger 2001-03
Bachelor of Science in Economics '13
Director of Product Support
Hoffman Equipment Co.
Residence - Long Valley, N.J.
Hometown - Andover, N.J.

There are days in everyone's life when you do not forget where you are at a particular moment. On September 11, 2001, the world stopped as terrorists launched attacks against our country. Athletic events were canceled all over the country. The Clemson-Duke football game was moved to December. Clemson's first opponent after 9/11 was home against Virginia on September 20.

The pre-game ceremonies for the Virginia game consisted of:
- A video message from Senator John McCain asking us to donate to the American Red Cross
- The names of all those killed scrolled on the video board to Bette Midler's "The Wind Beneath My Wings" and Simon and Garfunkel's "The Sounds of Silence"
- "America the Beautiful," "God Bless America," and "The Star-Spangled Banner" sung by a joint university chorus

Where was I located? I was standing on top of The Hill with an American flag. Everyone I spoke to during and after the game thought it was awesome that I ran the flag to midfield. Until this writing, no one ever knew I took the flag to every game in 2001, and I still have it to this day.

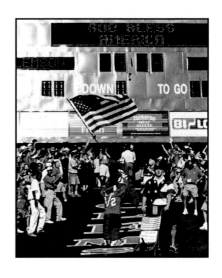

In the summer of 2002, I was sent to Los Angeles to film a commercial for Anheuser-Busch and the National Association of State Universities and Land Grant Colleges about safe celebration following sporting events. The commercial showed a coach giving his team a pep talk about being safe, as the camera panned around to the players and a group of mascots.

Everyone knows there are too many reality televison shows. During the fall of 2002, a reality show that was fun to watch was ESPN's "Beg, Borrow, and Deal." The show featured the one and only Clemson alumnus James "Bubba" Britton from Chester. So how do you get on a reality show? You are in an establishment across the street from Wrigley Field wearing a t-shirt from Sloan Street Tap Room (a Clemson business owned by Coach Frank Howard's son Jimmy), yelling at a friend with your Southern accent, when you are discovered.

This book isn't about Bubba (next to The Tiger), so you will have to Google the show. Bubba's team won the cross-country adventure. To celebrate the team's victory, Bubba and his teammates were invited to Death Valley to participate in one additional task: catching a 35-yard pass at halftime. They successfully caught the pass by former Clemson quarterback Rodney Williams on the first Thursday night game in Death Valley.

Final Score: #12 NC State 38   Clemson 6

Another important date was when The Tiger appeared at my wedding. My future wife Megan Nutt had no idea that Dan Licata would be in attendance in 2007.

BRAD STOEHR
No. 1 Tiger 2003-05
Bachelor of Science in Financial Management '05
Master of Business Administration '09
Queens University
Advisor Sales Associate Manager
Horizons Investments, LLC
Residence - Fort Mill, S.C.
Hometown - Spartanburg, S.C.

Legendary actor Jackie Gleason, aka Ralph Kramden in the sitcom "The Honeymooners" in the late 1950s, delivers one of the best lines of all time to his television wife, Alice. "One of these days, Alice, one of these days. POW! Right in the kisser! To the moon, Alice, to the moon!" I felt like I was going straight to the moon when I was selected as The Tiger. My aunt Katie Stoehr, Maryland class of '88, was Testudo, the Maryland student mascot, and she always told great stories about her time. So I wanted to join this elite group of students who have been their school's mascot.

Part of our tryout is how we interact with the fans. There is usually a baseball game on the day of the tryouts. I think the reason I won the job is that there was a high school team from Michigan that annually attends a game while on spring break. Their coach grew up in Pendleton. The music came on over the loudspeaker and I went over and started dancing with the team. The entire stadium turned and cheered us on. Thank you, Michigan.

My first appearance was at the Clemson BI-LO. I remember our advi-

sor walking up and I gave him a big hand shake. He then proceeded to take me by the snout and push me back and forth telling me what to do and what not to do. Simple instructions. Be yourself, be creative, have fun!

This appearance was followed up by attending a wedding at the Madren Center. I had only been The Tiger for a few weeks and had not remembered the code to the laundry room where the suit was kept. My girlfriend Leslie Miller, who became my wife in 2007, volunteered to climb through the chute and into a pile of dirty laundry so that she could open the door from the inside. Needless to say, I had to buy her dinner at Pixie & Bill's with my earnings from the wedding.

Final Score: Clemson 40   Duke 7

Bowden Bowl V was held on Coach Bobby Bowden's birthday. A special day in anyone's life. Each previous Bowden Bowl had been exciting games, win or lose. I made a sign that read "Wishing you a happy 74th birthday and a loss from Clemson. Go Tigers." It made it on ESPN that night.

Final Score: Clemson 26   #3 Florida State 10

Do I hold any pushup records? Yes, I do. I hold the record for the most pushups at an away night game (315) in 2003. The picture tells the story. A couple of weeks later I saw Coach Bowden and he asked me about all the pushups. I told him that I, along with probably 70,000 South Carolina fans, hated him for running up the score. He got a good laugh out of it. It's the one record I hope never gets broken unless we score 63 or more against the Gamecocks again.

Final Score: Clemson 63   South Carolina 17

There is nothing like beating the Gamecocks, but January 2, 2004 was a memorable night as the Tigers traveled to Atlanta and the Georgia Dome to play Tennessee in the Chick-fil-A Peach Bowl. Being on the stage and looking over the crowd and up at the stands after the game gave me goose bumps. I still get them thinking about that sight today. Thank you, Clemson fans, for your support both at home and on the road. You make special memories for a lot of players, coaches, and in my case, The Tiger.

Final Score: Clemson 27 #6 Tennessee 14

As good as 2003 and the beginning of 2004 were for any Clemson fan, 322 days later would be a black eye for Clemson and South Carolina fans. On November 19, the Indiana Pacers and Detroit Pistons were involved in a brawl at the Palace of Auburn Hills in Auburn Hills, Mich., with a minute left in the basketball game. The next day as the Tigers came running down the The Hill, their rivals were waiting for them in the end zone. If it hadn't been for the NBA brawl the previous night, many doubt that this copycat brawl would have happened. No need to go into detail other than it was Lou Holtz's last game as head coach of the Gamecocks, having gone 1-5 against Clemson.

Final Score: Clemson 29 South Carolina 7

Switching to the 2003-04 basketball season, my mother, Kathy Stoehr, was attending her first game. The Tigers were playing the North Carolina Tar Heels. I'm not exactly sure what she was thinking, but she showed up in a perfect Carolina blue-colored sweater. She isn't a UNC graduate, I just think she liked the color. The first thing my advisor did after seeing her was to go and get a Clemson t-shirt and give it to her. He said, "Your son is The Tiger, you have to wear orange!" She put the shirt on and wore it the entire game. After that, she always made sure to wear orange, just like fans do on Solid Orange Fridays or when attending an athletic event.

Although not in the suit, I proposed to my future wife Leslie at a basketball game. I had The Tiger bring me the ring, so that I could give it to her as announcer Dale Gilbert brought the crowd's attention to where we were sitting. I'm glad she said yes. It was a better location than next to the laundry chute. Married in 2007, we have two children, Stella Reese and Miller Patrick.

Final Score: Maryland 82 Clemson 66

While I never kept a letter of appreciation, I have a story that revolves around an appearance that I missed. I was booked for two events at the same time and didn't realize it, and I missed a child's birthday party. A year or so later, I was talking with a client, Brandon Cox, Class of '96, telling him about how I was The Tiger. He asked what years, and then he told me that I missed his son Will's third birthday! To this day, Brandon is still my client, but he never lets me live it down. A true Clemson family.

BRANDON LITTLE
No. 1 Tiger 2005-07

DAN LICATA
No. 1 Tiger 2007-08
Bachelor of Science in Secondary Education '09
History Teacher
Palmyra High School
Residence - Merchantville, N.J.
Hometown - Atco, N.J.

How many times did I try out prior to being selected? None. I actually became The Tiger before tryouts. I had transferred to Clemson from Seton Hall University in South Orange, N.J. where I was the mascot, The Pirate. Every once in a while a mascot burns out or may need to resign their position due to senior level classes. This was the case when the current Tiger mascot resigned to concentrate on his degree.

When spring came around, I tried out to be the official mascot. I had a great skit in which The Tiger needed to prove to his girlfriend, who had left him, that he still had the dance moves. I started dancing to "Working at the Car Wash" and "Splish Splash." The dances were purposely bad. I had recorded a female friend of mine saying, "That's all you got? I'll give you one more chance; otherwise, you need to go out with that Chicken from Columbia." Wow! The next song I danced to was "I'm Bringin' Sexy Back," which impressed his girlfriend, followed by her response of "Phew! You really are bringing sexy back!" He concluded with, "Cuz tonight baby...I'm gonna get freaky with you!" Finding out I was selected equated to the feeling I would have a couple of years later when I got my first job as a teacher.

After the skit comes the interview portion of the tryout. As a native of New Jersey, they asked me how I would react if someone called me a Yankee. In the costume, I would have ignored it. Out of the costume, I told them, "I am a Met, not a Yankee," referring to being a fan of the New York Mets.

Labor Day 2007 began with an appearance at the pre-game concert by Tiger Band in the amphitheater. The crowd there was electric. It was 91 degrees and I was like everyone else, going crazy. I never felt energy like that or at least I thought so at the time. On the parade down to the stadium, I thought we were going to enter the stadium by The Rock. As the parade continued past The Rock, I realized I had miscalculated the entrance and we were going to walk all the way around the stadium. I almost vomited in the suit from heat exhaustion. Upon reaching the end of the parade route in the west end zone, they informed me I had 40 minutes until kickoff.

I almost cried I was so happy and immediately started drinking Gatorade.

Thirty minutes later, I was headed east behind the Clemson bench to the top of The Hill. As the buses came around the north side of the stadium, my headgear began shaking. It was incredible. It was like standing on the deck of an aircraft carrier when an F/A-18E Super Hornet takes off.

After surviving the launch and cruising to a safe altitude around the 30-yard line, I turned around to look for #96 Jermaine Martin. We had spoken a few days before the game and orchestrated a jumping chest pump and three hand slaps. We were on a collision course when he stopped, and we pulled off our preflight moves. "The Most Exciting 25 Seconds in College Football" are more than that. They last a lifetime!

Final Score: Clemson 24   #19 Florida State 18

Seven weeks later, Central Michigan was in town for a noon game. I spent Friday night downtown with friends, figuring that the Tigers would have an easy time against the Chippewas. As the points piled up, so did the pushups. Clemson had moved into the 21st century by having more than one mascot work the games to prevent heat exhaustion. We switch every quarter.

In the suit for the first quarter, I only had to do seven pushups. My backup was Cory Luckett. Cory had to do 98 pushups in the second quarter after the Tigers scored four more touchdowns. A walk in the park.

Don't know if we had in the first, second, or third string players, but whoever they were made life rough for me in the third quarter as the Tigers scored four more times. Sadat Chambers scored on a 63-yard run to give the Tigers 63 points. The crowd went wild watching my shaky attempt at 63 pushups and a new record of 210 pushups in the third quarter.

Final Score: Clemson 70   Central Michigan 14

When the soccer-player-turned-placekicker Mark Buchholz hit the 35-yard field goal to beat the Gamecocks, I stormed the field to celebrate by running through those hedges in Columbia. The silence was deafening as the police escorted me through the home crowd. One fan lunged at me, but I stepped back. As he passed in front of me, a little Jersey attitude was in Williams-Brice Stadium that night as somehow my elbow was in the center of his back. Then I stepped over him and ran to the locker room.

Final Score: #21 Clemson 23   South Carolina 21

The 2008 men's ACC basketball tournament in Charlotte, N.C. was exciting. Coach Purnell's Tigers defeated Boston College (82-48) and No. 7 Duke (78-74) before losing to No. 1 North Carolina (86-81) in the finals. The two wins punched the Tigers ticket to the "Big Dance" and a trip the next week to the NCAA Tournament in Tampa, Fla. The Tigers would lose their first round matchup to the Villanova Wildcats (75-69) in Tampa; however, I will never forget the emotion shown by Clemson's Cliff Hammonds after the game. He was devastated after the loss along with many of my new friends in Tiger Band.

It felt like 100 degrees for the 2008 First Friday Parade. The annual parade is from the President's House to Historic Riggs Field and Dr. I.M. Ibrahim Stadium (named after former Clemson University President Walter Riggs and two-time national championship soccer coach Dr. I.M. Ibrahim, respectively). Getting to the stadium is easy. It's downhill, just like the "R.C. and Moonpie Downhill Mile" from the President's House to the Esso Club. Imagine what it was like to walk back through campus after the parade, amongst hundreds of people who want your picture, because you forgot to secure a ride back to your car.

After graduating in 2009, I applied for a teaching position at Palmyra High School in Palmyra, N.J. Clemson and my student teaching at Pickens High School had prepared me for this moment. As I looked across the table, there sat the principal, vice-principal and the head of the guidance department. They asked me to tell them a little about myself. I mentioned my 3.9 GPA in secondary education, volunteer work and baseball coaching experience at Daniel High School in Central.

When I concluded, the principal looked at me and said, "That is all great, but do you know why we brought you in today?" I was puzzled, until she pointed to the very bottom of my resume and asked, "Could you

tell us a little bit about this mascot experience?" I was floored. Her son was a high school mascot and wanted to continue as college mascot. I was hired two days later.

One of the most exciting days in any Clemson family life is the day the football schedule is released and you find out if your wedding day is during a home football game. If it is, you order televisions for the reception. Well, that was then; now all you have to do is look at your cell phone. Soon it will be your watch.

Former mascot Patrick Hitpass (2001) got married in Vineland, N.J. His mother, Joan, had the Athletic Department send the suit north and everyone got to dance the night away with the mascot.

One of the best days of my life was getting engaged in July 2015 to Sarah Calhoun. We are hoping that the 2016 football schedule does not conflict with our "big day."

NOLAN COLE
No. 1 Tiger 2008-10
Bachelor of Science in Electrical and
*   Computer Engineering '10*
Master of Engineering in Electrical Engineering '14
University of Idaho
Senior Engineer
Duke Energy
Residence - Charlotte, N.C.
Hometown - Asheville, N.C.

We are all told that someone is always watching you. Doesn't matter how big the venue. It's way more than putting on a suit. It requires a natural skill set, something you can't teach. You need an instinctive ridiculous side. Young kids will cry the first time they see The Tiger, because the parents didn't introduce their child to the Tiger Cub before The Tiger. Kids like the Cub's big shoes. When they get to be three or four years old, then they are ready for the main character. It's no different than Barney the Dinosaur or any of the kid shows on television.

Dogs and cats don't get along. During a parade, I felt a warm sensation. I looked down to see a poodle treating my leg like a fire hydrant. These aren't complaints; they are sacrifices that we make as we treat every appearance as if we are at a national championship game.

We wear a tuxedo t-shirt to weddings. The entrance is planned for the bridal party introduction, as everyone gets quiet and then you hear "Tiger Rag." At one wedding, after two hours I was walking back to my changing room. A door opened to a large auditorium, when a couple of high school kids grabbed me. All of a sudden, I was at a high school prom.

On another occasion, I was told to sneak up on a Gamecock groomsman and hit him in the face with a pie. Not a plate of whipped cream, but a legitimate pie. The laughter created for some great pictures. The groomsman was a great sport. I guess it all depends upon who wins the rivalry game.

While attending the Welcome Back Festival in downtown Clemson, a fraternity had made a slip-n-slide on Bowman Field. Before I knew it, about 50 people were yelling for me. When challenged, you have to accept. It was fun, but then I was covered with dish soap while still having to do my appearance. Everyone who hugged me for a picture said, "Ewwww, The Tiger is sweaty. But he smells nice!"

We are told to leave the field or court immediately at the end of the game, but we never listen. I was sweating so much it started dropping out of the mouth. This little girl in front of me got really scared and screamed, "Daddy, The Tiger is drooling, and he's going to eat me!" There was no convincing her otherwise.

Needing extra credits to graduate, I took classes in sign language and skeet shooting. The teacher who taught sign language mentioned that if you sign the National Anthem before a baseball game, you would get extra

credit. I approached him after class and told him I was The Tiger. Unlike Cocky who wears five-finger white gloves, ours are four-finger paws. I was the only student to sign in the suit. Thanks for the extra credit!

My best Halloween costume was when I dressed up as Quailman for the Coastal Carolina game. I wore a green vest, large underwear, a belt around the top of my head, and a shirt with a red

"Q" on the front. The people who didn't watch Nickelodeon didn't understand the costume, but it was great when the young kids and parents caught on and yelled, "Quailman!"

Have you ever been stuck to a wall? A furry suit and a Velcro wall at an elementary school field day do not go together. It took two men to pull me off the wall. After the appearance, I removed my head and started to unzip when I noticed a little girl, who couldn't have been more than six years old, looking straight at me through the window in the door. Next thing you know, her mom told her about the Easter Bunny, the Tooth Fairy, and a few other special characters. I guess all kids have to find out somehow.

Multiple appearance days are interesting, especially when you fall asleep in the suit at your second event. I was at a car dealership with eight cheerleaders when all of a sudden it started raining. There I was, out in the rain, catching a few zzzz's. Next thing I knew, they gave me a nudge; "it's showtime." I played it off lying there, but I got my batteries recharged.

Ever been to the Garrison Livestock Arena, located across Highway 76 from Tri-County Technical College? I got invited to a rodeo where a former mascot arranged to wear one of our extra suits while roping a calf on horseback. It was impressive. I was asked to go out in the middle of the arena and throw out t-shirts and footballs before they let out the bucking broncos. Suddenly, I turned into a rodeo clown or one of the Three Stooges who couldn't climb over the fence. End of my rodeo days.

My dad Rex and older brother Brody attended the Mascot Bowl during halftime of the Carolina Panthers-Miami Dolphins game. During the 15-minute game, I broke loose for a long run. Brody was running step for step with me along the sideline. The goal line was in sight when the Charlotte Bobcat ran me down with a tackle that knocked off my headgear. Suddenly the Charlotte 49er jumped on top of me to protect my identity, as the Campbell University Camel retrieved my headgear. Just like the mystery of who is Superman or Batman, my mascot fraternity protected my identity from the front page of the Charlotte Observer.

Parents are great, especially when your dad is a bee keeper and we are playing Georgia Tech. Dad

helped me make a bee keeper's veil for my headgear and gave me his bee smoker. Both a crowd favorite for a proud father. Thanks, Dad.

The only time mascots ever see the golf course is during charity events. Prior to the January 1, 2009 Gator Bowl against Nebraska, I did a promotional video for the game at the Players Stadium Course at TPC Sawgrass in Jacksonville, Fla. We all know about "Amen Corner" and the 12th green at the Augusta National Golf Club. However, the 17th island green at TPC Sawgrass is one of the hardest greens to hit. Ask some former Clemson golfers—Jonathan Byrd, Danny Ellis, Lucas Glover, Dillard Pruitt, Clarence Rose, D.J. Trahan, and Charles Warren, just to name a few. My ball ended up just like all those golf balls Kevin Costner hit in the water in "Tin Cup" before finally making the green. Hitting and staying on the 12th or 17th green are the biggest reliefs in golf.

Another challenge I accepted was prior to a basketball game at a ROTC pull-up contest. The leader had done 16 and I knew I could beat that total. I stuck my chest out and strutted up to the front of the line. As I started, I realized I didn't take into account the heavy suit and furry gloves. Needless to say, I got dogged by the crowd, but it got everyone pumped up for a good recruiting cause. Maybe I should stick to pushups. Ooh Rah!!

Each year, either on or close to Valentine's Day, the Rally Cats do a halftime dance with their boyfriend or a male friend. Like previous years, The Tiger is not invited to be a partner, which is disappointing. On this night in 2008, Erin Andrews was the sideline reporter. I approached Erin wearing my tuxedo t-shirt, holding a dozen roses, and a sign in my hand that said, "Erin, Will you be my Valentine?" We've been sweethearts ever since.

CHAPTER SEVEN
THE 2010s

MICHAEL SPEER
USAF 1st Lieutenant Michael Speer
No. 1 Tiger 2010-11
Bachelor of Science in Management '11
Deputy Program Manager
NETCENTS II Small Business
Residence - Montgomery, Ala.
Hometown - Mt. Pleasant, S.C.

Not too often The Tiger comes from the ranks of one of Clemson's prestigious Air Force or Army ROTC programs. My brother Andrew and I both received an Air Force ROTC academic scholarship to attend Clemson.

My family has a rich military background:

- My grandfather's cousin Captain Theodore "Dutch" Van Kirk was the navigator on the Enola Gay and flew on the mission that dropped the first atomic bomb "Little Boy" over Hiroshima, Japan which helped end World War II.

- My maternal grandfather, Rudy Bickel, was a military police officer (corporal) and a member of the Army of Occupation after World War II.

- My paternal grandfather, retired Lt. Col. Mike Speer flew cargo for the Air Force during the Vietnam War.

- My great-uncle, Jack Martz, was a lieutenant in the Army Air Corps and flew a P-57 during World War II.

- My father, Mike, a retired Air Force colonel, was a C-17 command pilot for the U.S. Air Force Reserves.

- My brother Andrew, Clemson Class of 2013, is a 2nd lieutenant acquisitions officer for the Air Combat Command in the U.S. Air Force Military Service.

- Currently, I'm a 63-A1 (acquisitions officer) in the U.S. Air Force as a 1st lieutenant. I execute the contracts for the Air

Force in IT support across the U.S. Recently I submitted an application to go to pilot training school for the Air Force Reserves at the Charleston Air Force Base.

While in the Air Force ROTC program, a decision heavily influenced by our family's military background, I first got an opportunity to fire the cannon while serving as a mascot. As my responsibilities increased as The Tiger, Andrew took over firing the cannon for the next three years.

Every Military Appreciation Day is special to those in attendance. On November 6, 2010, with Andrew in his utility uniform, more commonly known as fatigues, I stood behind him holding an American flag as four F-16s from Shaw Air Force Base flew over Memorial Stadium at the conclusion of the National Anthem. The first player off the bus holding an American flag was senior offensive guard Mason Cloy. Cloy was in the Army ROTC program at Clemson. "Duty, Honor, Country and Clemson Football" was our battle cry on this patriotic day.

Final Score: Clemson 14   #23 NC State 13

A young man with Down's syndrome heard that I was going to be at the Special Olympics at the Rock Norman Track on campus. The day I met this young Olympian was just as heartwarming as Military Appreciation Day. He drew me a Tiger Paw and was so excited to give it to me that his eyes were wet with tears. This in turn made me misty eyed, even though no one could see my tears. This Tiger Paw drawing is framed and hangs next to my Clemson diploma in my house.

A basketball mascot can have just as much fun with 8-10,000 fans as with 80,000 in Death Valley. It's hard to believe, however, at basketball games you get to be inside the pre-game huddle. You get to chest bump future NBA player Trevor Booker before he goes to battle.

The Air Force cadre knew, but my detachment did not know, that I was The Tiger. Prior to our senior photo, my teammates kept calling my cell phone and trying to get in touch with me. Not until they saw my name on the mascot website did they believe I was in the photo. "Ho ah!"

CHRISTOPHER "KIT" SOUTHWICK
No. 1 Tiger 2011-12
Bachelor of Science in Marketing '11
Area Director
Young Life
Residence - Columbia, S.C.
Hometown - St. Albans, Vt.

In 2009, Bellows Free Academy, in St. Albans, Vt., graduated two senior classmates who went on to become Division I college mascots. David Gagne was the lead handler of Ralphie, the live buffalo mascot at the University of Colorado, and I was the other.

Although not selected in 2009 as the No. 1 mascot, I was fortunate enough to assist with the program. On October 3, my family traveled to see me when Clemson played at the University of Maryland. It was embarrassing when my mom, Sue, shed her orange jacket. She was the only fan in the Clemson section dressed totally in black–an obvious fashion faux pas. It caught my attention and when my dad Dave came down to the field, I handed him an orange t-shirt and under my breath declared, "Have YOUR WIFE put this on." My younger sister, Addie, just finished her freshman year (2015) at Clemson, the third member of our family to attend Clemson University.

A great television sports announcer will go silent for up to two minutes after a special moment to allow the video to speak. Late in the fourth quarter, Florida State quarterback Christian Ponder threw an interception to Clemson's defensive back, Deandre McDaniel. Ponder then attempted to tackle McDaniel. However, McDaniel ran over Ponder, separating his shoulder. Standing over Ponder on the sideline pointing was Jay Williams, The Original Tiger Cub. A couple of plays later, we scored to guarantee the win. Tiger Band played "Tiger Rag" and then you could hear Queen's "We Will Rock You" over the sound system. Eighty thousand Clemson fans sang the chorus and with 30 seconds left, the guitar solo kicked in. It was a magical moment that will forever live on YouTube and cell phones. It was just like the words by television announcer Al Michaels, "Do you believe in miracles?" when the U.S. Hockey Team defeated the Soviet Union in the 1980 Winter Olympics in Lake Placid, N.Y. What a great night to be in The Tiger suit!

Final Score: Clemson 40 Florida State 24

Doing pushups is always fun, whether on the ground or being hoisted up in the air by the ROTC cadets. You never know when the day will come that you are setting a record. During the 2011 North Carolina football game as the No.1 mascot, I pumped out 225 in the third quarter, setting a record by 15.

Final Score: #8 Clemson 59 North Carolina 38

It had been 20 years (1991) since the Tigers won the ACC Championship. On this night in Charlotte, N.C., the orange sun turned into a real orange as the Tigers defeated the Hokies. It was raining oranges after the game as fans began throwing the oranges on the field signifying our championship and a trip to the Orange Bowl in Miami.

Final Score: #21 Clemson 38 #5 Virginia Tech 10

The Clemson-Carolina rivalry exists in just about every home in South Carolina. We've all seen the mixed marriage license plates and the car window flags. Family members don't talk to each for a year depending on the score. For example, Cocky and I were invited to a split wedding. I walked down the aisle with the groom holding the rings. Cocky was the maid of honor and the wedding took place in a funeral home.

We changed in the embalming room. I hope this was their family business.

The NFL Carolina Panthers host a Mascot Bowl at halftime at one of their games. I tackled Sir Purr in the first half, as the stadium booed. However, late in the second half, I took an end-around pitch for a touchdown giving the college mascots their first win and The Tiger the MVP Award!

It takes a special student to be a mascot. Until you show up for the tryout, you don't know if you can be that special person. This picture shows a Clemson student dressed in a red, white, and blue bodysuit at Military Appreciation Day. He could have been a good mascot. It really doesn't matter, as he is a true patriot! Semper Fi!

CHRIS ALSTON
No. 1 Tiger 2012-14
Bachelor of Science in Computer Science '14
Support and Infrastructure Engineer
KeyMark, Inc.
Residence - Greenville, S.C.
Hometown - Dacula, Ga.

Prior to graduation, the Alumni Association invites the mascot to attend an event so the graduating seniors can get one more picture with The Tiger. It was my first solo appearance and we were at The Rock, which is now inside a locked glass box. The seniors showed up not only for a picture, but for a chance to run down The Hill. It's a cool experience not knowing if you will fall or how high you can jump in the air as you go down The Hill. After the event, I found myself locked out of my changing room. Where is everyone when you need a key?

Gaines Adams, a 2006 unanimous All-American from Greenwood,

was the 2007 first round draft pick of the Tampa Bay Buccaneers. Gaines died from an undetected heart condition in 2010. This former Clemson defensive end was elected into the Clemson Athletic Hall of Fame in 2012, the first year of his eligibility. Gaines played football "For Love of the Game" (to borrow the name of a Kevin Costner baseball movie) and left a lasting impression on and off the field for so many fans.

There was a short video shown the night of Gaines's induction ceremony into the Clemson Athletic Hall of Fame at the Brooks Center. Gaines's video featured former South Carolina quarterback Steve Taneyhill talking about coaching Gaines in high school at Cambridge Academy. Yes, the same Taneyhill, who hit the imaginary home run and signed his name on the Tiger Paw in the middle of Death Valley. It was the first video of this emotional evening. Steve won the respect of all those in attendance. The rivalry and his antics were forgotten for at least 10 minutes as I presented Mr. Adams with his son's Hall of Fame award. It's the only time I ever cried in the suit.

You don't realize how special it is to be The Tiger. If you are a student at Clemson, please consider being a mascot. It's worth the time, energy, and more importantly, the memories. Do it "For Love of the Game." At the end of your "movie," you get to wear the mascot gloves at graduation.

The easiest pushup record to set is the one for the first quarter. All you have to do is score a touchdown each and every time you get the ball. But, it is hard to have more than four possessions. However, on November 3, 2012, the Tigers scored a touchdown on each possession. The record number of first quarter pushups was set at 70 on this special Saturday afternoon.

Final Score: #10 Clemson 56   Duke 20

Since divisional play began in 2005, the 2012 season marked the first time the Tigers ever tied for first in the Atlantic Division, and then did not get to play in the ACC title game due to the loss to Florida State. With the bad comes the good, like the win on New Year's Eve followed by watching the peach drop in Underground Atlanta. A pretty good night for the $2 Tiger Paw bill to be strewn by Clemson fans. It's a tradition started in Atlanta in 1977 to show the economic impact of Clemson fans attending away games.

Final Score: #14 Clemson 25   #9 LSU 24

ESPN's "College Gameday" was in Tigertown in 2013 for our game against the Seminoles. The Goodyear Blimp was parked at the Oconee County Regional Airport and ESPN invited me to participate in the pre-game pep rally, flying above the crowd in the co-pilot's seat. Unfortunately, the morning fog grounded the air ship, just as the Seminoles later grounded the Tigers. Now you know how we prepare to do pushups prior to a game.

Final Score: #5 Florida State 51   #3 Clemson 14

The final game of the season was at the Discover Orange Bowl and Sun Life Stadium in Miami Gardens, Fla. on January 3, 2014 against the Ohio State Buckeyes. Florida State had won the ACC championship, and was selected to play Auburn for the Bowl College Series national championship in Pasadena, Calif. This allowed Clemson to represent the ACC in the Orange Bowl. The Tiger Cub and I were selected to dot the "i" during Tiger Band's pre-game performance.

Final Score: #12 Clemson 40   #7 Ohio State 35

Once at an appearance, Sir Purr, the Carolina Panthers mascot, showed up wearing power stilts. It was the coolest prop I had seen someone use. A poor college student can't afford the power stilts, so I purchased a cheaper plastic version. Adding two feet to my six-foot frame caught the eyes of the basketball coaches and players as I bounced around Littlejohn Coliseum. I remember once an opposing coach saying, "Hey! He wasn't on the scouting report!"

A knowledgeable college basketball fan knows the history behind the National Invitational Tournament. As a player or coach, all you want is another game. Although the 2013-14 season didn't end with a trip to the NCAA Tournament, it did end in New York, playing Southern Methodist University and Hall of Fame Coach Larry Brown in the semifinals.

Basketball tournament games are the worst! You are confined to a small area with the cheerleaders and/or dance team, and you cannot move unless instructed. While I enjoyed the prestige of being at The Garden, I did not enjoy the game because you could not move along the baseline or go up in the stands. Like the Road to the Final Four, the games leading up to New York were worth every second in the suit.

Final Score:

Clemson 78	Georgia State 66	First round
Clemson 50	Illinois 49	Second round
Clemson 73	Belmont 68	Third round
SMU 65	Clemson 59	Semifinals

ANDREW BEELER
No. 1 Tiger 2014-15
Bachelor of Science in Management '15
Residence - Clemson, S.C.
Hometown - Greenville, S.C.

My roommate, Collin Stokes, and I were at a football game during our first semester in the Clemson Bridge Program in 2011. He brought up the idea of being the mascot and that sparked my interest.

My first time running down The Hill was on Military Appreciation Day in 2013. Next to me was Daniel Rodriguez, a Purple Heart recipient and true hero, waving an American flag. I waved an Honor and Remember flag. A patriotic moment for any American.

Final Score: #7 Clemson 52   The Citadel 6

In the summer of 2014, I traveled to Louisville, Ky. along with mascots from all the ACC schools for an event welcoming the University of Louisville to the conference. We got a behind-the-scenes tour of the Hillerich & Bradsby Company. The company has produced the Louisville Slugger baseball bat since the turn of the 19th century. We also visited Churchill Downs, which opened its doors in 1875 to host the first Kentucky Derby.

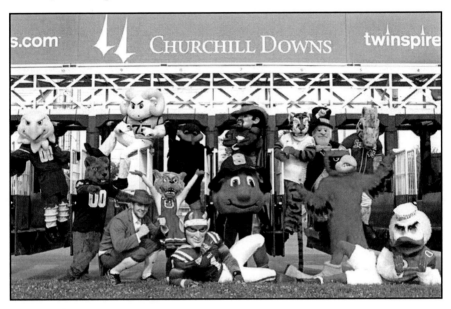

Not since my sophomore year of high school had Clemson beaten South Carolina. The losing streak was up to five and now it was my senior year at Clemson (2014-15). Going into the game, I wasn't sure how quarterback Cole Stoudt would fare against the Gamecocks. We never had to find out, as quarterback Deshaun Watson, playing with a torn ACL, led us to victory. There were no more talks about a possible "6-peat." The stars and planets were back in order.

Final Score: #23 Clemson 35   South Carolina 17

There are no official records for the number of appearances by a mascot. However, between December 2012 and August 2014, I made a total of 218 appearances, with another year to go! Looks like 300+ will be the unofficial record.

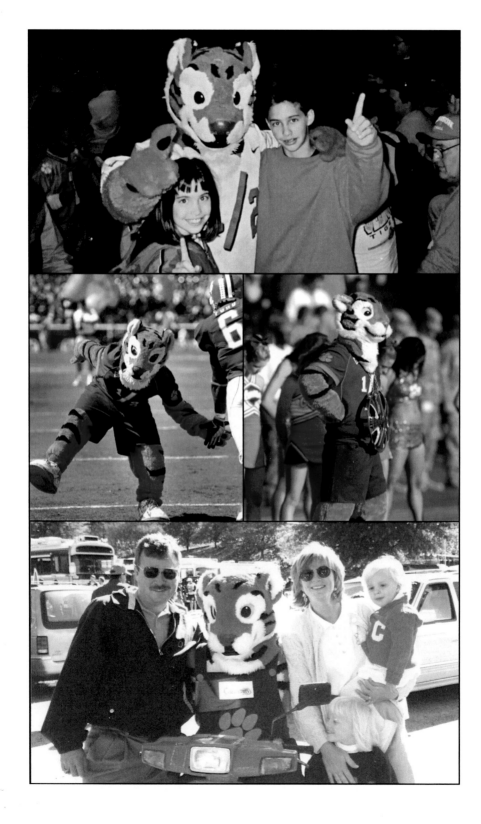

CHAPTER EIGHT
THE TIGER CUBS

JAY WILLIAMS
The Original Tiger Cub 1993-95
Bachelor of Science in Management '91
Master of Human Resource Development '94
Master of Education in Counseling,
  and Guidance Services '96
Sales Representative
Quiksilver
Residence - Annapolis, Md.
Hometown - Fairfax, Va.

In July 1993, the Clemson Athletic Department decided to add a new mascot to support IPTAY's Tiger Cub Club. The purpose of the club was to get the loyal fan base to enroll their children into IPTAY at a very young age.

Children up to 18 years of age could become members of this newly formed youth group. Parents had the option to pay yearly dues from $30 to $250 for their first 18 years. Today, the 18- to 22-year-old students attending Clemson can become members of the Collegiate Club. After graduation, the Collegiate Club members are then invited to become members of IP-

TAY as first-time donors, carrying on a family tradition.

The Athletic Department began looking high and low for someone to be their new mascot, the Tiger Cub. They got lucky because *I had nothing to do.* I was already in graduate school, working at Manifest Records, bartending at The Gameroom, and DJing at WSBF radio. An administrator had stopped by The Gameroom and was talking to Mike "Snake" Casey, one of the owners, after work one day when my name came up. Next thing you know, we were on the road to the costume design company, Scollon Productions in White Rock. Our design for the Cub costume looked like a Walt Disney character: big shoes, coveralls, friendlier face and shorter than The Tiger.

The Tiger Cub was introduced as the nephew of The Tiger. How would the two mascots interact with each other? What would the fans think of another mascot?

It's safe to say the rest is history. The Cub is widely accepted by young children who are sometimes afraid to walk up and hug The Tiger. The big shoes, friendlier face, smaller size, the walk, and the oversize t-shirt have all added to the Cub's personality. POW!

On Saturday, September 23, just like the Chick-fil-A slogan – "Home of the Original Chicken Sandwich" ~ the Original Tiger Cub made his debut. I popped out of the backseat of the 1963 Checker taxi cab on the 20-yard line, driven by Caroline Stewart, along with her nine-year-old son Elliott, who was acting like a chauffeur for my grand entrance. It was a successful day for the Tigers and the beginning of a new era of Clemson mascots.

Final Score: Clemson 16   Georgia Tech 13

After a 7-3 regular season, Head Coach Ken Hatfield resigned and Tommy West was hired to coach the Tigers against Kentucky in the Peach Bowl on the eve of 1994. At half time, The Tiger and I were looking for a place to cool down and recover when we ended up in the back of the Clemson locker room. We sat on the floor in a back hallway, heads off and suits pulled down to our waists. For the first couple minutes we just sat there drinking water and then we realized we could hear the coaches talking to the team. We both looked at each other and said, "This is pretty cool..." You often wonder what a coach is going to say to his team at halftime. Like the team, we were pumped up for the second half.

The end of that game may have produced the biggest emotional swing and exciting moment I experienced while wearing the suit. Clemson was down six and driving when quarterback Patrick Sapp threw an interception to Kentucky's Marty Moore. I remember when I saw that pick my heart sank...seconds later, after Moore tried to return the interception, Clemson's Rodney Blunt stripped the ball and Brent LeJeune recovered the fumble. New Life! What a swing of emotions. A few plays later, Sapp connected on a 21-yard touchdown pass to Terry Smith to tie the game. Nelson Welsh kicked the extra point to send the Clemson fans to Underground Atlanta to watch the giant peach drop celebrating the win until the early morning hours. What an unbelievable finish.

Final Score: #23 Clemson 14   Kentucky 13

As a mascot alum, I was on the sideline for the 2009 Florida State game in Death Valley. Clemson was up 33-24 with 3:43 left in the game when Florida State's Christian Ponder dropped back and threw an interception to Deandre McDaniel. As I watched McDaniel return the interception, I saw him point for a block. I looked and realized he wasn't calling for a block, he was pointing to Ponder who was coming to tackle him. McDaniel lowered his shoulder and cracked Ponder. That literally happened five feet in front of me.

On Monday, I saw this YouTube link with me pointing at Ponder: https://www.youtube.com/watch?v=pfI6UZ8pwP0

Not WOW, but POW, what a moment!

Final Score: Clemson 40   Florida State 24

In the spring of 1994, it was required that I try out to be the Cub. This was a strange experience since I was the Original Tiger Cub. What was my feeling once I was formally selected to be the Tiger Cub? I was a little anxious, but it was time to get back to normal, as I was tired of others wearing MY suit during the tryout.

BRIAN GERHART
No. 1 Tiger Cub 1995-96
Bachelor of Science in Parks, Recreation
and Tourism Management '97
Residence - Arlington, Va.
Hometown - Silver Spring, Md.

Homecoming '95 was a pristine morning and my custom-made tux had just been pressed. I suited up and hopped on my shiny, red scooter, cruising through East Campus, Bowman Field, down Highway 76 and along Perimeter Road. Seeing everyone's reactions while beeping my horn and waving was a real thrill. Before the game, I drove the scooter onto the field with The Tiger on the back.

There was a time when friends would ask me, how did I get that scar on my head? It happened during my first-ever attempt at a back flip that landed me square on my head. It didn't seem bad at first. My embarrassment was concealed in the suit. After a few minutes my eyes began to sting as blood began to stream down my face. I had managed to split open a decent portion of my forehead from the stunt gone wrong. But with so much adrenaline pumping, I got patched up quickly and returned to the court to continue entertaining the crowd. The hazards of being a mascot.

The last time, to my knowledge, anyone saw a

Clemson mascot not in full uniform (other than President Jim Barker), happened at the Winthrop Coliseum in Rock Hill when I was interviewed by *The State* newspaper during the 1996 ACC Women's Basketball Tournament. Sorry, everyone.

Later that spring, I flew with members of the football coaching staff to an IPTAY meeting in Virginia. As the day progressed, the coaches did their thing, and I did mine. Then it was back to campus. I'll never forget the breathtaking view flying back to Clemson with the sun setting over Lake Hartwell, and the sky resonating orange and purple tones beyond the Blue Ridge Mountains.

RYAN TETEN
No. 1 Tiger Cub 1996-98
Bachelor of Arts in English and
*   Political Science '99*
Doctoral degree in Political Science '04
Vanderbilt University
Department Head, Political Science
University of Louisiana Lafayette
Residence - Lafayette, La.
Hometown - Richmond, Va.

At a football game in 1995 while watching the Tiger Cub, I told my roommates, "Before I graduate, I am going to do that." The next spring, I had applied to be a residence hall advisor. The day I walked down to the Jervey Athletic Center for the mascot tryout, I found out that I was not going to be an advisor. However, that night as I put on the Cub suit, I knew I was going to be selected. One door closed and another opened.

Most of our travel to away games had been with Tiger Band. But in 1996, the band did not go to Columbia, Mo. for a game against the Missouri Tigers. The mascot advisor grew up 45 miles east of St. Louis and was driving to the game. The Thursday prior to the Saturday game, Mike Bays, The Tiger, and I jumped in his car and rode to Nashville, Tenn. for an alumni event with former mascot Stuart McWhorter ('91). On game day, Truman The Tiger and some Mizzou band members came after The Tiger and the Cub with an aluminum baseball bat, grabbed us, and ran us into the goal posts. I know that you are supposed to let the other mascot win in their stadium, but that was unacceptably brutal. It was the last time we went by mascot protocol.

Final Score: Missouri 38 Clemson 24

Florida State rolled into Death Valley in 1997 ranked fifth in the country. Fans expect antics from the mascots. So we dressed up as cowboys since we were playing a bunch of Indians (Seminoles). Our props were silly string, super soakers, and holsters. During the game, we accidentally sprayed a group of sorority girls in sun dresses. The combination of the water and silly string painted on the white dresses made them look like rainbows. Sorry, girls.

Final Score: #5 Florida State 35   #16 Clemson 28

A year later, Testudo, the Maryland student mascot, and two friends tried to have an actual fight with me. Our cheerleaders held his two friends, and I, having wrestled at the 125-pound class at Manchester High School in Richmond, Va., performed a three-point throw of that giant turtle. His head came off when he landed. He didn't come back to our side to mix it up for the rest of the game.

Final Score: Tiger Cub 3   Testudo and Friends 0
Clemson 20   Maryland 9

Being a mascot during the Rick Barnes basketball era was awesome! Coach Barnes's Tigers finished the 1995-96 season by upsetting No. 20 North Carolina 75-73 on a Greg Buckner dunk as time ran out in the first round of the ACC Tournament.

Expectations for the 1996-97 season were high as the Tigers opened up the season at the RCA Dome in Indianapolis. The Tigers met the Kentucky Wildcats in the second game of a doubleheader. Game one saw Coach Bob Knight's Indiana Hoosiers beat Coach Jim Calhoun's UCONN Huskies,

68-61. After Indiana's win, The Tiger and I came out wearing Indiana t-shirts to show our support for the local team. It was a great move because the Indiana fans ended up cheering for Clemson.

Final Score: #20 Clemson 79 #3 Kentucky 71 OT

After defeating Kentucky, the Tigers won 15 of their next 16 games to reach a No. 2 national ranking in late January. The season however ended with a double overtime loss to third-ranked Minnesota in the Sweet 16 of the NCAA Midwest Regional Tournament.

Final Score: #3 Minnesota 90 #14 Clemson 84 2OT

The 1997-98 season started off fast with an 11-2 record heading into the New Year. March Madness is crazy for everyone; however, as much fun as it was in 1996-97, the end of the next season was harsh on the Tigers in the Windy City of Chicago. The Tigers were upset in the first round of the NCAA Tournament by Western Michigan, 75-72. No matter how high your expectations, when you lose, the NCAA sends you home as soon as possible, either that night or early the next day. We spent one afternoon in The Madhouse on Madison, home to the Chicago Blackhawks, the Bulls, and former Tiger All-American Horace Grant, who had been the No. 1 pick of "Da Bulls" and a four-time NBA champion.

Usually the mascot surprises fans by going up to girls, hugging them, and just messing around. On a spring afternoon, while working a baseball game, I found what would be my "diamond in the rough." I unknowingly pretended to propose to a girl (Tonya) while in the suit. After she played along, she whispered to me to come back and talk when I finished. I thought that was pretty brave, not having any idea what was underneath the headgear. I found out later that night that she had scoped me out at a previous game--so it wasn't as big of a risk as I thought. I did go back to talk to Tonya, and we have been married since 1997. We lost the game to California 12-10, but I won the girl of my life and the mother of our children, Aidan and Seth.

DAN WANGERIN
No. 1 Tiger Cub 1998-01
Bachelor of Science in Marketing '01
Sales Manager
Weruva International
Residence - Atlanta, Ga.
Hometown - Sheboygan, Wis.

BI LO has been the Exclusive Grocery Store for Clemson Athletics for over 25 years. In early 1998, then BI LO President Jon Wilken approached Clemson Athletics with designs for a new store in Clemson. The creative Wilken and his staff presented drawings with the Tiger Paw incorporated in their logo. In addition, there would be pictures of coaches, former great players, clothing items, and other logos that branded the BI LO consumer to Clemson Athletics.

It didn't take long for Clemson to agree to this unique theme store to promote its brand. Six months later the store opened with a ribbon-cutting ceremony with representatives from Clemson Athletics, BI LO, and city leaders in attendance. The store was Solid Orange even before the athletic department began its Solid Orange campaign in the early 2000s.

Customers attending the grand opening were treated to many specials. None, though, were as special as the items they received from the Tiger Cub and The Tiger. As we walked up and down the aisles greeting people, we grabbed random items and placed them in people's carts when they were not looking. During checkout they had the greatest looks on their faces as they were unloading the carts. Most people thought it was funny when they saw us laughing.

In the spring of 1999, Coach Jim Davis's Lady Tigers basketball team was playing the University of Illinois in the second round of the NCAA Tournament in Littlejohn Coliseum. It was the first meeting between the two schools.

At halftime, the Illinois mascot, Chief Illiniwek, portrayed by a student dressed in Sioux regalia, performed a native Indian dance. At the conclusion of his performance, the Illinois fans yelled, "Chief!" as he marched off the court.

Then I walked on to the court to present my version of his dance. It wasn't until I got into the tunnel that I found out from my advisor (who had completed a graduate internship at Illinois), how sacred of a dance I was imitating. Although funny, it was inappropriate to mock The Chief.

The University of Illinois retired Chief Illinwek on February 21, 2007, after 81 years of performing at halftimes of football and basketball games and volleyball matches.

Final Score: #10 Clemson 63 Illinois 51

During all three years I was the Tiger Cub, the Lady Tigers were in the NCAA Basketball Tournament. In 2001, while in Cincinnati for the first and second rounds, the cheerleaders and I went to the Rock Bottom Brewery for dinner. Who walked in but none other than Nick Lachey, from the music group 98 Degrees, and his brother Drew. All the girls went crazy trying to be cool and totally failing. All I was hoping for was to see his fiancée and future wife, Jessica Simpson.

Final Score: #12 Xavier 77 #22 Clemson 62

Baseball season was always fun for me, especially during rain delays. It looked easy, so off I went as I began to crawl underneath the tarp that was covering the infield. My goal was to crawl all the way under and come out the other side. I quickly found out how heavy the tarp is and having water on it made it worse. I made it about 10 feet before getting lost. A couple of minutes later I finally made it out by first base. A soaking wet suit was my next problem. The $3,500 suit I was wearing was green from the chemical they use on the field. Luckily the equipment manager knew how to remove the stain from the suit.

Water always seemed to get me into trouble. The next time I was at the McHugh Natatorium in the Fike Recreation Center. As if I didn't learn from the baseball game, I jumped off the high dive at a swimming meet. It was by far the dumbest thing I ever did. As I hit the water, the headgear I was wearing did not go under water so it almost ripped my real head off. Next, the suit got super heavy real fast from the water. There I was struggling to get to the side of the pool and shimmy up the ladder to climb out.

For someone from Wisconsin, getting to meet fans and being "adopted" by them was one of the greatest things about being a mascot. I'd like to give a special shout-out to Jack, Nancy and Tootsie, Andy and Laurie, and Rick and Diane. Thanks for showing me what "There is Something in These Hills" truly means.

KATE WEPPNER
No. 1 Tiger Cub 2001-02
Bachelor of Science in Marketing '04
Architectural Review Board Administrator
Palmetto Dunes Property Owners Association
Residence and Hometown - Hilton Head
Island, S.C.

My first experience with Clemson Athletics was on the diamond field as a batgirl for Coach Jack Leggett's Tigers in 2000. It was Coach Leggett's third trip to the College World Series at the helm of the Clemson baseball program.

It's not known who the first Clemson student was to put on The Tiger suit. What we do know is that Jay Williams was the first Tiger Cub in 1993. We know that Clemson Agricultural College opened its doors in 1889. We know it became a co-educational college in 1955. We also know that in 1963 Harvey Gantt was the first African-American student to enroll in Clemson.

In 2001, I became the first female mascot when I was selected to be the Tiger Cub. That summer, I attended the cheerleading and mascot camp held in Myrtle Beach. While there, ESPN taped a segment of the Georgia Tech mascot and me out of uniform. They blurred our faces to conform to the theme of the segment, which was on mascot confidentiality, that aired on ESPN's "College Gameday" in late September when we played at Georgia Tech.

Final Score: #25 Clemson 47 #9 Georgia Tech 44

One of my worst experiences was traveling to the University of Maryland where my brother Michael was a senior. After the game had started, I ventured over to the Maryland student section, knowing that my brother was in the front row. While messing with their mascot, out of nowhere their mic man body checked me from behind. He hit me so hard my headgear flew off and it knocked the wind out of me. You could tell he felt awful when he saw he had body checked a female. The student section laughed when I stood up, put my head back on, and kicked the mic man in his private parts.

Final Score: #13 Maryland 37 Clemson 20

The final first as the Cub for this Kappa Delta sorority girl was when the Clemson University Parking Services had my car towed before a basketball game with my suit in the trunk. Upon discovering my car being towed, Parking Services was nice enough to take me to the impound lot to retrieve it. It was the last time I left the suit in the trunk of the car.

My husband, Tim Nolan, and I currently reside on Hilton Head Island.

JORDAN POWELL
No. 1 Tiger Cub 2002-03
Bachelor of Science in
*   Graphic Communications '05*
Realtor
Keller Williams Realty
Residence - Greenville, S.C.
Hometown - Chesnee, S.C.

I found out about tryouts in a pretty random and funny way. I lived off campus and my apartment was across the street from where several football players lived: Woody Dantzler, Rod Gardner, and Robert Carswell (to the best of my memory). Nick Eason visited the other players on a regular basis.

While talking to Nick, I told him I would give anything to run down The Hill. He recommended I walk on the team as a kicker, but after seeing my skills, or lack thereof, we both knew that would never happen. A month later, we were downtown when Nick pointed out the mascot advisor to me. I introduced myself, and he said tryouts were starting in a few weeks.

At the end of tryouts, I was disappointed and surprised when my name was not called. I found out I would have been selected had I not used a little foul language when answering the question, "What do you think it would be like leading the team down The Hill?"

All I had to do was use a different verb or adjective. You think the judges would have understood my excitement. Who doesn't get excited when you see the buses come around the stadium by Fike and pull up to the backside of the scoreboard? Your blood is pumping, just like the blood of the coaches and players getting off the bus. Then all of a sudden, you hear the first note from Tiger Band. A minute later, the cannon fires as 80,000 fans are screaming at the top of their lungs. We've all been to that boiling point of excitement.

Long story short, a year later I understood the importance of our body language and the words we use every day, especially when you are representing yourself, your family, and the Clemson Family. It took longer than expected; however, it was worth the wait to be a part of the "Most Exciting 25 Seconds in College Football."

Prior to the tryout, we were told to do anything to stand out and entertain the judges. I went BIG and started out with the Dolly Parton song "9 to 5" as I strutted in wearing a deep V-neck t-shirt with two footballs stuffed inside. After shaking my Tiger tail, I ripped the tee shirt at the neck and tossed the footballs to the judges. It was the beginning of "Hulkamania" (a term used by professional wrestler "Hulk" Hogan) for me as I would be running wild the next year as the new Tiger Cub.

By the way, you don't realize how hard it is to remember parts to your suit, especially when you go to an appearance as either The Tiger or Tiger Cub. It's like going to the grocery store and getting home and you forgot the milk. It's that feeling that you left the house open or your clothes at home. What do you do? You pull over the car and check your travel bag to see if you have both gloves and a pair of shoes. It's kind of hard to forget the head or body.

While heading to a wedding in Charleston, I got that dreaded feeling, and I was right. Problem was I was already in Summerville. I improvised by running into a store and grabbing a pair of orange hunting gloves. I don't think anyone ever realized. Just like when I did an appearance in flip-flops or dress shoes.

When you get married you have to ask for permission to do anything. If you are a mascot, you ask for forgiveness. My fiancé Angela Winstead and I were married in the Upstate in 2010, but wanted to do something special for our wedding photos. So we decided to have our photo shoot on our honeymoon in Playa Mujeres, Mexico. The Tiger suit has only been out of the country twice, when the Tigers played in Tokyo in 1982 and 1991. On the fourth day of our trip, I had the pool boy José at our resort dress up in the suit. He was 16 or 17 and was outgoing like most mascots. As you can see from the picture, everyone is smiling which hopefully is good for one future kitchen pass.

In 2004, the current ACC mascots went to Fox Sports Channel in Charlotte, N.C. to film a commercial welcoming the new mascots to the ACC. They were Boston College's Baldwin the Eagle, Sebastian the Ibis from the University of Miami, and the Virginia Tech HokieBird. We all tried to be professionals; however, when you get 12 mascots together over a two-day period, tensions do run high at times. It all started when Sebastian was flashing

his 2001 National Football Championship ring. Then Buzz from Georgia Tech started doing what he does best, poking around in everyone's business, while being annoying.

We weren't on "Tobacco Road," (the term used when you go play Duke, North Carolina, NC State, and Wake Forest), but close enough for the Duke Blue Devil and the North Carolina Rameses to take a break from studying and start talking basketball, as if anyone cared. The Wake Forest Demon Deacon and the Virginia Cavalier were nowhere to be found. They were last seen complaining to the caterers about not having any wine and cheese in the break room.

Finally, I had enough and left the room to find Florida State's Osceola so we could tell the new mascots that the ACC was about football. It seems that Osceola had the same thought, as I found him putting on his makeup in the restroom. The HokieBird was in the stall with an upset stomach. The fowl bird must have eaten some bad food or drank out of the wrong punch bowl.

The Tiger was a man alone in this crowd of goofballs, especially after finishing the 2003 football season with a 63-17 win at Williams-Brice Stadium and with a Gaffney Peach-sized beat down of the Tennessee Volunteers (27-14) in the 2004 Peach Bowl. Feeling full of confidence, The Tiger got everyone straightened out. It was an interesting 48 hours in the Queen City of Charlotte, to say the least!

On a serious note, Rameses was an outgoing young man named Jason Ray who everyone loved being around during those two days. A few years later, Jason died after being hit by a car while in New Jersey for the NCAA Basketball Tournament, just hours before he led his beloved Tar Heels onto the basketball court. Jason had a profound impact on many people on "Tobacco Road" and around the country – none more than the four lives he saved by being an organ donor.

After you have stopped reading some or all of this book, please go to the internet and watch the video "Ray of Hope" about the lives Jason saved. It's hard not to think about Jason when you see the Tar Heel mascot, Rameses. For more information about Jason Ray's foundation, visit www.jasonray.org.

It's easy to put on the suit and entertain the crowd at a sporting event, parade, wedding, etc. What you can never be prepared for is when you visit a person in the hospital. I met Ben Jordan and his father one afternoon at the Greenville Children's Hospital. Ben was in the 11th grade and played football at Belton-Honea Path High School in Anderson County.

I was told by Kenneth Jordan that running down The Hill as a member of the Clemson football team was one of Ben's biggest dreams. Ben passed away almost 24 hours after my visit. I never imagined his death was so near. God put me at the right place at the right time to be able to lift Ben's spirits in his final hours. I attended Ben's funeral. The Jordans said my visit meant so much to Ben and the family. Ben was told he would never be able to play football again. With my hand gestures and sign language because I can't speak while in character, I was able to tell Ben he could still run down The Hill, not as a player, but as the mascot. He smiled and laughed. His parents told me after I left until his passing his spirits were lifted as if he was his old self, a happy-go-lucky teenager.

Losing anyone in your life is difficult, but the news of Ben's passing has affected my life. I guess it's a combination of Ben being a young man with so much life ahead of him, or our mutual love for Clemson University and the Tigers. I, like all mascots, appreciate the platform we have to impact so many lives. We know our visits help with a patient's recovery in ways that today's medicines and technology can't. Who knows, maybe a Tar Heel- -Jason Ray–was in the room on this special day in Ben's life.

PAUL HUGULEY
No. 1 Tiger Cub 2003-05
Bachelor of Science in Economics '05
Children's Minister
First Baptist Spartanburg
Residence – Spartanburg, S.C.
Hometown – Myrtle Beach, S.C.

No one knew for five months that I was the new Tiger Cub until I told my family I was going back to Clemson for Fan Appreciation Day. I didn't know how to zip up the suit by myself until I found an equipment manager and off I went to the stadium. To solve my uniform problem, I attached a lanyard to the zipper. Thirty minutes into the event I was dehydrated because I just had my wisdom teeth removed and was suffering from dry socket. I hid in a ticket booth for an hour until I had the energy to get back to Jervey gym. A couple of hours later I was at my apartment when I began vomiting from trying to rehydrate. At 2 a.m., I called a friend to take me to the emergency room where I received my first IV for dehydration. The next morning the administration called me wanting to know why I missed Fan Day.

A month later, we were hosting Middle Tennessee State University when a photographer told us that some fans near the Blue Raiders locker room wanted pictures. The Tiger took off first towards the fans when all of a sudden a flying horse, Lightning, popped out from around the corner. He was a two-legged horse mascot with wings. He began to shove The Tiger around not knowing that we had two mascots. When I caught up with them there was a loud "whoo" from the west end zone fans, much like when an opposing quarterback gets "Vic Beasley-ed," "Brian Dawkins-ed" or "William Perry-ed." One of Lightning's flying wings had come off his costume.

Final Score: Clemson 37   MTSU 14

Working the Georgia Tech game with Mike Bays, who was substituting for Brad Stoehr, broke the ice for me getting comfortable in the suit. Late in the game I pulled out a giant fly swatter made from foam board and a broomstick. I pretended to swat at the Tech students in the first row. Suddenly, Buzz came from nowhere and snatched the fly swatter. He broke the stick over his knee and the student section went crazy. Carrying

the pride of Clemson University, I knew this was unacceptable. I got a full head of steam and speared him to the ground. We got back up and I speared him again. He got smart and twisted on me, so I twisted back for a third slam to the ground! Buzz then broke character and said "That's enough!" Monday morning I received a reprimand from the administration. An Atlanta news station had videoed the takedown.

Final Score: Tiger Cub 3   Buzz 0
Clemson 39   Georgia Tech 3

The Tiger was putting "Clemson Beat Maryland" stickers on Maryland fans by pretending to pat them on the back. The Terrapin came over, and they started staring each other down as I got on my knees behind an unknowing Testudo. The Tiger pushed the turtle, who tripped over me--a routine that you often see mascots perform. Just like in "Animal House," we were put on double secret probation after someone from Maryland complained to the administration.

Final Score: Maryland 21   Clemson 7

The next week, I ran up to find my grandparents in their seats in the lower deck (I think UI) and sat with my grandmother. She was wondering why the Cub had come up the stands to see her. They were suspicious as to why I was sweaty and late getting to their tailgates after the games. I gave her a hug and took off down to the field for the 4th quarter.

During the 63-17 win at South Carolina, I went into the locker room at halftime. Derrick Hamilton was looking at me sweating and asked if I was worn out. He scored the first of nine touchdowns for the Tigers on a 36-yard pass from quarterback Charlie Whitehurst in the first quarter. Derrick left the room and quickly showed back up with a Gatorade bottle for me from his locker. I felt honored that I had received rehydration from one of the stars of the game.

I made a horse for the Florida State game in Tallahassee in 2004.

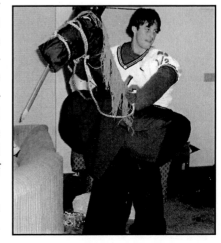

My legs were the front of the horse with fake legs hanging down in the back. My left arm controlled the head while a fake left arm went to the reins. My right arm was free to hold a spear with a Clemson flag on it. I had all intentions to run out on the field and throw the spear down mocking Chief Osceola. As I stepped out of the locker room, the equipment manager stopped me and said my costume would start a fight. I regret that I listened. Coolest prop that never made it to the field.

Final Score: #8 Florida State 41   Clemson 22

For the final game of the season, I had a fishing pole with a chicken on the end. During South Carolina's halftime show, I cast the chicken out towards their band members and then reeled it back in as I sat leisurely in a lounge chair in the east end zone. On this day, the Tigers caught 15 passes. A good day on any lake if you ask Clemson public address announcer weather forecaster, and avid fisherman, Dale Gilbert.

Final Score: Clemson 29   South Carolina 7

Wearing a red nose and antlers, Rudolph made an appearance at a holiday basketball game to see who was naughty and nice before Santa made his delivery to all the young Clemson fans.

A rain delay and a baseball tarp are a mascot's dream prop. I started running and sliding on the tarp one day. Fans and players were jealous that I was using this giant slip-and-slide to have fun. It wasn't until May 17, 2011, during a 30-minute lightning delay in the first inning between Clemson and Davidson College had two teams come together to entertain the hundred or so fans in attendance. Their skits were instant classics on YouTube, just like Abbott and Costello's "Who's On First" skit. Look them up, they are guaranteed to make you laugh.

The Tiger and I were invited to a Greenville Growl hockey game with other local mascots to play broom ball between periods on the ice. We couldn't keep our feet and were falling all over the place. The Wofford College Terrier came to me wanting to perform a stunt of a dog chasing a cat. I think he was a little confused, thinking that I was a cat and not a Tiger. As he chased me, I turned and planted my foot on top of his, causing his shoe to come off. Everyone had a good time checking each other into the boards as we tried to score goals with our brooms. It all ended with a huge dog pile in the middle of the ice!

One of my professors was holding a reading club in Pendleton. She picked me up at my apartment. She couldn't find a parking spot so she parked on the side of the road, and we went to read to the kids in the park. A policeman stopped by and began writing her a ticket. I walked over in my suit, took the pen and pad out of his hand and waved to him not to write the ticket. He asked if it was my car, and I nodded "yes." He told me to move it. I waved OK and returned his pen and pad. It saved my professor a parking ticket. I need to check my transcripts and see what grade I received that semester!

ESPN unexpectedly filmed me at the Florida State game in 2003 as I was doing "the Worm." Eighteen months later they had me fill out a waiver. Before I knew it, I was in the 2006 EA Sports NCAA Football video game doing "the Worm" to "Tiger Rag."

It was a great honor to represent Clemson University. I still carry this honor with me every day, along with meeting players and the coaches that I had watched on television growing up. I got teary-eyed during a moment of silence for Jim Phillips, the "Voice of the Tigers" for 36 years (1968-2004) prior to the Middle Tennessee State game. The "Dean of ACC Announcers" had passed away 10 days after announcing his 400th football game on August 30th when the Tigers hosted Georgia. His 1,000th men's basketball game was during the 2002 ACC Tournament. I never got the chance to meet Jim; however, I was present for the salute by Tiger Band.

CLINT CAGLE
No. 1 Tiger Cub 2005-07
Bachelor of Science in
 Mechanical Engineering '07
Master of Science in
 Mechanical Engineering '09
Mechanical Engineer
Electrolux, North America R&D
Residence - Concord, N.C.
Hometown - Canton, Ga.

Of all the Tiger Cubs, I consider myself the prop king! My favorite was a nerd outfit with a giant calculator, nerd glasses, and a sign that read, "Got Nerd?" at Bobby Dodd stadium. I held the sign up as a shield and walked in front of the Georgia Tech student section.

Another was a plumber outfit with overalls, plunger, and a sign that read "Cleaning up the Duke-y."

Sebastian the Ibis, the Miami mascot, did not like the bag of bread that I was throwing at him. He was a "foul" bird.

At NC State in 2005, I dressed up as a pirate captain because they had elected a student as student body president who called himself The Pirate Captain. Funny that he won on a platform dressed as a pirate since East Carolina's mascot is Pee Dee the Pirate and that's their rival.

At basketball games, I had a giant inflatable basketball that I would try and shoot in the basket and then pretend to get frustrated when I couldn't make it.

I also had a giant stuffed fish and fishing net that I would always carry around. Don't know why, maybe because Lake Hartwell is next to campus.

The second year for tryouts I dressed up as a caveman. My poster read, "Beating USC, so easy a Caveman could do it," after a popular GEICO commercial at the time. Then I attempted a handspring but failed to properly

strap the headgear on, and the head went flying off. Playing Cupid is self-explanatory.

After one of my two First Friday Parades, President Barker graciously invited me into the White House (President's House) and said, "Relax, make yourself at home." He is the commander-in-chief of the university so I proceeded to follow orders, raid the fridge, and take a shower.

Speaking of headgear, I tripped running down The Hill once wearing a new Tiger head. It bounced up so I couldn't see, causing me to miss the transition between The Hill and the field. I completed the fall by doing a somersault. The football players knew what had happened, and were laughing as they passed.

The song lyrics about New York say, "If I can make it there, I'll make it anywhere, it's up to you, New York, New York." I wasn't in New York in 2006 when I made a half-court shot during halftime of a game but in Little-john Coliseum. However, I got to shoot in "The Garden" during the final two games of the 2007 National Invitation Tournament. A very memorable moment, considering Madison Square Garden is the most famous arena in the world.

Final Score: Clemson 68 Air Force 67 Semifinal
West Virginia 78 Clemson 73 Championship

The coolest birthday party I went to was when some parents created a football field in their back yard complete with lines and goal posts. It was Clemson versus South Carolina with Cocky and myself as quarterbacks. I felt like Charlie Whitehurst (4-0), Steve Fuller (3-0), Homer Jordan (3-0) and Clemson's first football Academic All-American, Charlie Bussey (2-0). Don't know what the final score was, but I assume that Clemson won. As a matter of fact, I know we won! Going into the 2015 season, Clemson leads the series 66-42-4.

I attended the mascot reunion in 2014 but, unfortunately, was not on the field. I happened to be sitting in the stands with probably a couple of other former mascots. This shows how important it is to keep your information up to date with the Clemson Alumni Association, IPTAY, and the Block C Club. As Forrest Gump would say, "It Happens."

Brooke Murphy, my girlfriend of two months, asked me to come in character to her dad Steve's surprise 50th birthday party. When it came time to ask him for his daughter's hand in marriage, Steve said "Yes." We've been married since 2010. (If this part doesn't make the book, then I know I will be left out of my father-in-law's will.)

TYLER ALEWINE
No. 1 Tiger Cub 2007-08
Bachelor of Arts in History '09
Technician
Access Garage Door
Residence - Seneca, S.C.
Hometown - Greenville, S.C.

December 2007 saw the Tiger Cub in Jacksonville, Fla. for the induction ceremony of the newest class of ACC Football Legends at the Jacksonville Municipal Stadium. You are saying where? The Alltel Stadium sponsorship had expired after the 2006 season so the stadium went back to its previous name from 1995-96. I know it's confusing. Why didn't they just go back to calling it the Gator Bowl?

Like most college students, we don't drink enough water, so I was dehydrated prior to my appearance. The medical staff at the Gator Bowl set me up with an IV underneath the suit. I had the bag taped to my back and kept my arm at a 90 degree angle the entire night as I escorted Clemson's Jerry Butler into the Hall of Fame. Jerry was the recipient of the spectacular catch (known as "The Catch 1") in Clemson's 31-27 win against South Carolina in 1977.

Usually rehearsal dinners and weddings are easy events. You meet a soon-to-be Clemson couple or you surprise one half of the family that are Carolina fans. One rehearsal dinner had just five people in attendance, and I was hired for an hour and a half. There was no DJ. They pointed at me and said "You are the entertainment!" That was the last time I did not ask prior to an event what was expected of my appearance.

When I was a mascot judge a few years ago, we asked a student why he

wanted to be the Cub. He described a basketball game when he was in middle school that made him and his family laugh. We then asked him what year, and he said 2007. That's when all the judges realized it was one of my events. It was pretty comical.

After graduation, I wanted to transition from a collegiate mascot to a minor league mascot and eventually to the big leagues. Finding employment with any team is a challenge that requires working multiple jobs in order to earn sufficient income. I ended my search by accepting a position as a therapist at Northside Elementary School in Seneca while working as a mascot for the Greenville Drive. The Drive is a Class-A affiliate for the Boston Red Sox with Reedy Rip'it the Frog as its mascot. I was also Rowdy, the mascot for the Greenville Road Warriors, an affiliate of the New York Rangers and Philadelphia Flyers hockey teams. After three years, I moved to the beach and was employed by the Myrtle Beach Pelicans in the community relations department. The Pelicans were a Class-A affiliate at the time with the Texas Rangers, and I was Splash, one of their two mascots; the other being Rally Shark.

No matter the team, my vision of a mascot was a funny, child-like character who could entertain fans from ages 8 to 88. I strove to create an atmosphere that fans would never forget while they escaped from a hard day at work. In the suit, I was able to push boundaries and act as crazy as I wanted while getting paid to do it. I would go down slides on the playground with children, give random fans kisses, and goof off with the older men by shining their bald heads or rubbing their big bellies. All in good fun.

After putting on a scene, I removed

the suit for a break and walked past the fans that I'd just interacted with and went unrecognized. They had no clue I was the mascot as I went from the center of attention to a typical staff member in a matter of seconds. In time, I built relationships with season ticket holders who became my friends. They supplied me with Gatorade, gum, snacks, etc...I would shoot them with silly string, throw popcorn on them and take their souvenirs to give to other fans. It was all a part of the experience in creating my character. From supportive season ticket holders to rowdy children, the fans truly are a part of your family.

In addition to entertaining the fans as a mascot, I was responsible for facilitating in-game activities. My dressing room was a kid's heaven with countless oversized toys and props like the t-shirt cannon that looked like something from "American Gladiator." With the help of a Gator, we drove around the ballpark shooting 30 t-shirts in 15 seconds.

Appearances can be emotional. I had the honor of visiting an elementary-aged girl who was a big Clemson fan. She could light up the room with joy. Victoria was in a coma on the day of my visit and passed away a couple of days later. When asked my most memorable appearance, it's being a member of Team Victoria. God bless all those battling cancer.

At the Pelicans, I worked with schools, businesses, and non-profits. I created a school incentive program called MVP. Each classroom had a poster with a baseball diamond. At each base, teachers set goals for students to master. Upon completion, students were rewarded by our sponsors and received a complimentary ticket to a game. At the game, students played with the mascot and participated in a pre-game parade to recognize their accomplishments.

The Pelicans and I also participated in the schools' state testing preparation by hosting pep rallies in the weeks prior to the state achievement tests. Our street team played games on stage with students and teachers and talked about test-taking strategies. In addition to the school, the baseball team also partnered with an organization called Backpack Buddies, which provided food to students in need with our Make a Splash program. Every Monday, fans who donated goods received a complimentary ticket and an autographed baseball card that noted each player's community service. The program raised over $400,000 in its inaugural year.

Other organizations we partnered with included the Grand Strand Technical Council and Horry County Special Olympics. The council taught students engineering by creating a Splash Pelican mascot robot. It was the

first robot to throw a pitch of 70 mph at a sporting event in South Carolina. Special Olympics allowed for special needs students to enjoy a day at the park with a party, donut eating contest, and a chance to run the bases. At the end of the event, these special athletes were invited on the field to watch fireworks with Splash. We raised over $16,000 the first time we held the event.

In order to audition to be a professional mascot, it's important to constantly recreate the character, send videos and network. Making contacts and connections is vital because there are no postings for jobs in the newspaper, on Craigslist, or Linkedin.

In my journey to become a professional mascot, I placed 11th in the nation out of all the minor league mascots and was offered a Triple-A position by the Charlotte Knights, an affiliate of the Chicago White Sox. I declined so I could spend more time with my family.

What started out as a childhood dream in Death Valley became a reality and then a career. It ultimately taught me that the mascot is more than just a person in a suit. I learned about life.

The Paw says it all. To the Clemson Family, I am forever grateful.

MARTIN DREW JERNIGAN
No. 1 Tiger Cub 2008-09
Bachelor of Arts in Philosophy '09
Park Operations Coordinator of Attractions
Walt Disney World Resort
Residence - Windermere, Fla.
Hometown - Cope, S.C.

It's not how you start but how you finish. The 2008 season started off with a 3-3 record. After a coaching change and a home loss to Georgia Tech just five days in his new position, Coach Dabo Swinney then had 14 days to get the Tigers focused for a road game at Alumni Stadium in Chestnut Hill, MA, five miles away from Fenway Park in Boston. Alumni Stadium hosted the 1969 Boston Patriots just like Memorial Stadium did in 1995 for the Carolina Panthers in their inaugural NFL season.

Prior to the game, Baldwin the Eagle and I decided to meet in the middle of the end zone. We started in the sumo stance and placed our hands in front of each other. We than had an intense best two out of three rock, paper, and scissors match. Baldwin won the battle that day, but the Tigers got their first win under their new interim head coach.

Final Score: Clemson 27 Boston College 21

There are many people you thank on your way up the ladder to success. I have to give credit to my high school librarian, Lynn Garrick, for my first appearance as the Easter Bunny at an event for our pre-school. Just like Coach Swinney, you don't always succeed at your first attempt; however, I did become the Cub on my third attempt.

After graduation in 2010, I headed south to the Walt Disney World Resort in Orlando, Fla. The NC State Wolfpack was playing the West Virginia Mountaineers in the Champs Sports Bowl. A couple of days before the game, the Pack was visiting the theme parks. I was working at the EPCOT attraction called Mission: Space when Russell Wilson and three teammates came through the single rider's line. He pulled me towards him and tried to use his influence to get all four of them in the same ride. My response was simply, "Go ACC! I'm a Clemson grad, and I'm not putting all of you in the same vehicle. Rules are rules. Go Tigers."

He walked into the loading zone, as directed by another cast member, with a slight smirk on his face. Russell would lead State to a 23-7 win. Hey Russell, I thought in 2015 you would have learned how to bend the rules and hand the ball off. You might have been named the MVP and won a free trip back to Disney World with your teammates.

Employees who work at the Disney Resort meet people from around the country and world. I had become friends with a photographer who was a fan of the Miami Dolphins. He brought me a flyer about their mascot tryout being held at the Hard Rock Café Hotel and Casino in Hollywood, Fla.

Decked out in Clemson gear, I entered the tryout room and answered the basic interview questions followed by random scenarios that had nothing to do with football. The entire process lasted about 20 minutes.

Three weeks later, I received a phone call for an interview with the head of cheerleaders and entertainment at Sun Life Stadium. The interview consisted of a live crowd performance as T.D., the Dolphins mascot, at an elementary school to promote the Play 60 campaign.

A week later, I was one of two selected to appear at each home game, all while still maintaining my job at Disney. As T.D., I stood next to Head Coach Tony Sparano, kissed the hand of Kim Kardashian and met the GEICO Caveman. The Dolphins won one home game in 2010; however, I got to see them play against Tom

Brady, Ben Roethlisberger, and Ndamukong Suh, along with former Tigers Chris Clemons and Phillip Merling. My time as the Cub at afternoon games prepared me for the Miami heat.

SARAH NEWBURN
No. 1 Tiger Cub 2009-12
Bachelor of Arts in Special Education '12
Special Education Teacher
Washington Junior High School
Residence - Westmont, Ill.
Hometown - Port St. Lucie, Fla.

Having just completed a five-mile run around Perimeter Road, I was heading to Harcombe Dining Hall when I got a text from Tyler Alewine reminding me about tryouts. I was tired, hungry and didn't want to go. My boyfriend at the time and future husband, Collin Chavous, continued towards Harcombe as I went to the Jervey Athletic Center. When I walked in, there were all these boys wearing athletic clothes. I wasn't ready for this until I saw Tyler. He gave us the inside scoop on what to expect.

Next, everyone had the joy of meeting the advisor, and he scared me to death. After a brief introduction, he disappeared and Tyler told us to suit up. I said, "Wait, what? Suit up? Now? I thought this was just an interest meeting?"

I was the second person in the suit wearing a sweater and blue jeans. My Steve Madden shoes were replaced by the larger Nike shoes worn by the Cub. With my long blonde ponytail hanging out of the suit, I went to the baseball game running up and down the walkway, kissing babies, eating popcorn, and rubbing bald heads.

Dancing to the music and cheering on the Tigers, they had to keep tucking in my pony tail (I later invested in a swim cap). It was difficult to see, hard to walk, and the suit dragged on the ground. Not sure what I looked like from the outside, but on the inside, I was smiling. I loved every minute of it and felt like this was going to be my new hobby. Hard to believe I almost didn't go. I was drenched in sweat, but I didn't care. I wanted to be the next Tiger Cub.

My first official appearance as the Cub was at Clemson's Relay for Life. They talked me into wearing the sumo wrestling inflatable suit and smashing into other wrestlers. As if it wasn't hard enough to walk, I was completely exhausted after about two minutes. After that, I walked with football players and took pictures with the sorority girls who were trying to get me to hold up their sign. The mascots do over 300 appearances a year. Each appearance is different; however, those that raise money for charities are special.

Everyone forgets a part of the suit, and it usually happens when you are making an appearance off campus. The car I had wasn't very reliable, so I drove to Pickens and picked up my mom's car. Halfway to Charlotte, I remembered the entire suit was in the trunk of my car. I called my mom, and we met by the Greenville-Spartanburg International Airport. The second and final time I had to adapt was at a wedding when I had only one glove. I wrapped my hand in an orange Clemson t-shirt and a hair tie and kept it behind my back in all the pictures.

One of the unexpected rewards is seeing yourself in a commercial that airs during football games on television. The fall after I graduated, I was in a commercial wearing my cap, gown, and gloves. Graduation is the first time many of your classmates realize that you were a mascot. We worked hard to keep our identity a secret. This wasn't the case during the early years of The Tiger.

The ACC mascots have a Facebook page which allows us to keep in touch with each other. Once, I met up with the Demon Deacon after a game for dinner. Another time, Buzz was coming through Clemson after a business trip and stopped for lunch. When time permits, we smack-talk via text messages right before we play each other.

Your props define your character and everyone has an alter ego. The Tiger dressed up as Captain Underpants and I was Superman during a Halloween game against Coastal Carolina. Against Wofford, I walked around with a pet carrier that said "Free Puppy," and the students began yelling, "No one wants that puppy, it's not potty trained."

One of the traditions that Coach Dabo Swinney brought back to Clemson was walking to the stadium. Today it is called Tiger Walk. Prior to the locker room being built underneath the stands of the west end zone, the Tigers used to walk from their locker room in Fike Fieldhouse to Memorial Stadium. To play my part, I went to Goodwill and purchased a tuxedo, complete with pleats. With a hole in the rear for the tail, I was properly dressed for each walk with the team.

In 2011, Auburn was riding a 17-game winning streak which included their 2010 national championship. Next to the indoor practice field is a graveyard that has tombstones representing road wins over programs who are ranked in the Top 25 at the start of the game. Prior to the game, I found a gravestone that had a skeleton on it with red eyes that lit up and said "RIP." I added – "Win Streak Buried in Death Valley," and that's what happened.

Final Score: Clemson 38 #21 Auburn 24

The next week, I bought a sign with Dabo's saying "Shock the World Tour" from Clemson Variety and Frame. The Tiger and I unveiled our signs when we got to the top of The Hill. It was the beginning of another "We Will Rock You" evening.

Final Score: #21 Clemson 35 #11 Florida State 30

Quarterback Tajh Boyd had gotten injured because he was not wearing his hip-pads at a game. The next week he came back and I was wearing hip pads on the outside of my suit with a sign that said:

   √ Swag
   √ Hip Pads
   √ 8-0

until C.J. Spiller checked it off in front of the student section once we secured the win.

Final Score: #8 Clemson 59   North Carolina 38

Everyone knows The Tiger does pushups after a score. Not on this occasion when he was switching places with another student. I just happened to be standing by the pushup board when we scored. The ROTC cadets were slamming their hands on it and looking at me. I looked at the scoreboard and saw a 17 and told myself, I can do this. The hard part was keeping my balance while wearing the size 28 shoes. It was a lot of fun, but I was thankful it was only 17. It was the last time I ever did pushups.

Mascots are entertainers with athletic ability, which means we do get hurt. I tore a ligament in my knee jumping over the wall after Jacoby Ford caught a 26-yard game-winning touchdown pass from quarterback Kyle Parker. The overtime catch helped the Tigers beat the Miami Hurricanes 40-37, in 2009.

Going to Chapel Hill proves they are a basketball school. They didn't have anywhere for us to change prior to a football game. Nowhere!! We had to change in the locker room with our football players. I remember Andre Ellington being shocked to see that the Cub was a female. Fans and especially students should not assume that the Cub is always a male. It's funny when the girls hit on you.

The biggest birthday party the Cub attends every year is the one the kids throw for the Cub early in the football season. Thank you for the cards and crafts you give to the Cub each year. It is very much appreciated.

Prior to the 2009 ACC Football Championship in Charlotte, all the ACC mascots went to a Harris Teeter grocery store. It was a terrible idea to let us run around with no supervision. I grabbed a bag of kitty-litter and rode the checkout conveyer belt. Then the Hokie mascot joined us, and we grabbed some turkey legs and put them in the cart. We finished the appearance by racing electric scooters throughout the store.

After misbehaving at the grocery store, all the ACC mascots became very professional at a local children's hospital in Charlotte. It was time to bring joy to some very special youngsters.

To finish off the championship weekend, I had the privilege of escorting Coach Danny Ford onto the field during the ACC Football Championship game. He was being recognized as an ACC Legend.

Former Head Track and Field Coach Bob Pollock used to have a dinner prior to Christmas where his student-athletes purchased gifts for needy families. Giving can be contagious, and it spread even more when Head Basketball Coach Oliver Purnell started Tiger Winter Wonderland. At this event, the basketball coaches and student-athletes provided even more gifts for area families. It's always special when you are a part of giving back to the community, especially those in need.

Collin and I currently live in Chicago as he is attending dental school. When I heard about the reunion in 2014, there was no way I could miss it. We drove through the night to be there. It was fun meeting the Original Tiger Cub and swapping stories with the other mascots. During our introduction, the mascots went into character even though we were not in uniform and began doing pushups. It gets into your blood the first time you put on the suit, and it never leaves.

As I look back, what did it mean to be the Tiger Cub? Saying it was an honor doesn't even do it justice. It's the greatest experience I've ever had, until I got married to my husband, Collin, of course. To be a member of this fraternity is incredible, and I share this honor with my brothers as we have a bond that is unexplainable. We are the face behind The Tiger head, and we know what it means when someone says, "There's Something in These Hills."

KACIE TROJANOWSKY
No. 1 Tiger Cub 2012-13
Bachelor of Science in Health Science '13
Pharmacy School
University of South Carolina
Residence and Hometown - Lexington, S.C.

It's tough when you leave home for college and have to make your own decisions. My parents were not as excited as I was when I told them I wanted to be the Cub. Since they were paying my tuition, they cautioned me about how much time it would take from my studies. That didn't stop me, though. My heart was set on my first real decision. My family was right beside me every step of the way, even at all the games.

During my interview, the judges asked me my name, and I pointed to the back of the Cub jersey. They asked me again as they instructed me to take off the Cub head. I shook my head "No!" Then I realized I was supposed to have an interview being myself. I had been stubborn, but that is one of the mascot rules: Do not talk when in character.

My first appearance as the official Tiger Cub was an engagement photo shoot on the football field. I'm not going to lie, it was really awkward holding hands with a couple while they kissed in front of me for the picture. Luckily, the Cub has a permanent smile on his face.

The engagement picture was not as bad as another wedding where the mother of the groom, who was a non-Clemson fan, started to strangle me. She was not joking around. Luckily I got out of her grip and was able to steer clear of her the rest of the evening.

The first time you run down The Hill is exciting and, like most players, you don't think you need to practice. However, when the cannon goes off, you almost have a heart attack! I managed to complete the run without falling and getting stomped on by the football team before I did my version of the Lambeau Leap. There I was on the wall in front of the student section as I caught my breath.

Working a volleyball match was fun, but the steps are so close together in Jervey Gym that I always found myself tripping because of the big shoes. Luckily, the crowd loved it. I knew I was going to fall, so I made it look dramatic. It's in the small venues that you learn to perfect your skills and motions.

Although I was never in a television commercial, I was with the cheerleaders for a video that played on the football stadium video board concerning litter around campus. I got to jump out of a recycling bin and dance around. Solid Green is what keeps Clemson a beautiful campus. Thanks, everyone, for supporting this campaign.

My roommates knew that I was the Cub, but I never told my friends. Just like when I did not talk during my interview, I tried to keep my identity a secret.

SAMANTHA CAMPBELL
No. 1 Tiger Cub 2013-14
Bachelor of Arts in Biological Sciences '14
Science Teacher
St. Charles Borromeo Catholic School
Residence - Orlando, Fla.
Hometown - Lexington, S.C.

Coaches are always ready for a challenge and like to talk trash. So Dabo, are you sure you want to challenge me? Do you really think I'm one of your lineman? Get a real job and stop pestering me. I see you imitating every step and motion I am making. If you want to be the Cub, and not The Tiger, due to your size, then attend the next tryout which will be held the week after spring break. I'm sure they will be glad to have you as the next Cub. Good luck!

My one and only time working the ACC Women's Basketball Tournament Fan Fest was the worst and funniest thing that happened to

me in the suit. I started interacting with a group of kids when someone, I never saw who, hit me hard square in the back. It knocked the breath out of me as I fell forward. I started breathing rapidly until I found one of our handlers. They helped get me back to the change room where I remembered I had left my mascara on. Imagine what I looked like half dressed in the suit with the head off and mascara running down my face! I looked like Elaine in the 166th episode of "Seinfeld" known as "The Strike" or the "Festivus" episode. When the other mascots saw me, they didn't know whether to laugh or cry, I looked so ridiculous.

You know how proud your parents must feel when both of their daughters dress up like furry animals. Honey, look what we raised! My older sister, Kristin, was Clyde the Cougar at the College of Charleston and because of my height, I tried out and was selected as the Cub. We had the greatest time walking around historic Charleston in our suits on a beautiful summer day. It made the South Carolina slogan, "Smiling Faces, Beautiful Places" truly come to life.

On my next trip to the Lowcountry (the area of South Carolina along the coast line below Myrtle Beach toward Hilton Head Island), I visited a friend at the Medical University of South Carolina who was recovering from major heart surgery. It doesn't matter who the mascot is, it is our responsibility to distract patients and family members, to bring a brief smile to their faces. Following the visit I walked around the pediatric wing to visit sick children. Some of them had never heard of Clemson, let alone the Tiger Cub, but you could see the happiness that came from a visit from this silly little Tiger. During the past few years this girl with a child's height got to play the role of a lifetime as if on Broadway. Thank you, Clemson!

Hollywood celebrates the Oscars, Broadway has the Tonys, music has the Grammys, and Clemson has the Clemmys. This event celebrates Clemson's student-athletes' achievements in the classroom and on the field of play. If it's in Clemson, it's only appropriate for The Tiger and Tiger Cub to make a grand appearance on the Orange Carpet for a photo op.

During my senior year, I met President Jim Clements at the Discover Orange Bowl and spilled my Cub identity to him. He always remembered me after that night and would hug me every time I saw him around campus or at games. On graduation day, as I approached

him wearing my cap, gown, and holding my diploma, I was ready for that first hug as a proud Clemson University graduate!

LAUREN ADAMS
No. 1 Tiger Cub 2014-15
Bachelor of Arts in Biological Sciences '15
Residence - Clemson, S.C.
Hometown - Irmo, S.C.

This is a picture of me visiting Madelynn over the Christmas break in 2014 when I was a back-up Tiger Cub. She was diagnosed with Stage 4 neuroblastoma cancer in November 2013. The future was unpredictable for her, and she told her parents a

visit from the Cub would make her happy. Through connections with my mom, I was able to go visit her twice in the hospital, the latter a couple of weeks before she passed away. She was a huge Clemson fan and fan of the Tiger Cub. The nurses said her visits with the Cub were some of the only times she smiled or laughed while in the hospital.

The first year I tried out, I was selected to be the back-up Cub. Whether you are the No. 1 or backup mascot, you are a symbol of Clemson. Kit Southwick influenced me to try out and without him I would have forgotten and been too nervous to go by myself. My skit began with "Here Comes the Boom" by Nelly. I had placed a mini trampoline by the door inside Jervey Gym and during the introduction of the song, I came out, bounced on the trampoline and danced to the song. This quickly transitioned to "What Makes You Beautiful" by One Direction and using a flower I had made out of poster board, I danced with a cheerleader. I gave her the flower on one knee. Next I had a South Carolina fan pull on my tail. I played tug of war with him and won. I held up a tombstone of the Gamecocks' upcoming demise in November and another poster stating "Undefeated Dance Party." I danced to "Wop, Jump on it, and 2 Step" and finished with "Tiger Rag."

During the interview, they asked me to state my name while in character. Mascot Rule No. 1, do not take the head off in public. Rule No. 2, do not talk while in character. Good Cub!

My first appearance was in Tillman Auditorium at the graduation ceremony for students in the Clemson LIFE program. LIFE means "Learning Is For Everyone," and it is a college program for students with disabilities. The students learn life skills that include academics, employment and social skills. This event was a rewarding experience. It allowed me to see a side of the university that most students never encounter.

One of the highest honors any Clemson graduate can have is to be able to dot the "i" prior to a game. This honor is usually given to the mascots during bowl season. The Tiger and I were given this privilege prior to the 25th anniversary of the Russell Athletic Bowl in Orlando, FL.

Final Score: #18 Clemson 40   #24 Oklahoma 6

CHAPTER NINE
NO. 2 TIGERS

BRADY CHATELAIN
A Cajun Tiger
Bachelor of Science Psychology '11
University of Louisiana Lafayette
Master of Healthcare Innovation
Arizona State University '13
Data Quality Coordinator
Compass Health
Residence - Lafayette, La.
Hometown - Hessmer, La.

In 2009, the Clemson Athletic Department was looking for someone to wear their Tiger suit for a wedding reception in Lafayette, La. At that time, I was Cayenne, the student mascot for the University of Louisiana Lafayette. When Clemson reached me, I said it would be a honor to represent their university. The groom-to-be was Don "Truck" Hymel, a Clemson football administrator, who was getting married to Dana LaPointe. In attendance would be many of their friends from the Palmetto State.

There are always surprises at a wedding or reception. The young ring bearers may stop walking towards the altar when they see their parents or it could rain at the outdoor reception. "Always expect the unexpected" is a good motto.

Every wedding has a rehearsal and that's what I did the same day when the suit arrived in the Bayou State. Each uniform is different, just like a tuxedo. After making a couple of adjustments, I rehearsed my walk and motions in front of the mirror while listening to the "Song That Shakes the Southland." Tiger Rag!

It's not our custom in Louisiana for a college mascot to attend receptions. However, this was a Clemson man getting married. The mascot had to be in attendance. And the food had to be Cajun, just like the food–jambalaya, gumbo, and a good old-fashioned Louisiana-style crawfish boil–Truck served at the Cajun Café, the platform area of the baseball stadium in Clemson.

Let it be said, the real Tiger and not Mike the Tiger (the LSU student mascot) had quite the presence in Lafayette on this October evening. Ahh Eee!!!

RUDY GILL
No. 2 Tiger 1987-88
Bachelor of Science in Management '88
Senior Vice President
Tidelands Bank
Residence - Mt. Pleasant, S.C.
Hometown - Oxford, N.C.

It didn't take me long to learn you should never underestimate the opponent. Georgia Tech had made the trip up I-85 for a game in Death Valley, and I was the big man on campus. Why not? I was in The Tiger suit. During the game, I went over to mess around with Buzz when he grabbed and flipped me. I was a little stunned, but fought back. After a couple of minutes of tussling, I invited Buzz over to the mascot area under the mic man platform where we could take our heads off and rest. Buzz was a petite girl. I didn't tell anyone for a couple of years.

After the game, when I was back in my room, my dad, HT for Horace Thomas, called to tell me our family and friends got a huge laugh when the television announcer Roman Gabriel commented that he "sure would like to see the body of that person in the suit." I was so small and thin that I wore "spider" shoulder pads underneath the suit to fill it out. Another suit adjustment I needed was orange shoe strings to tie the legs up so they wouldn't drag. Six years later the Tiger Cub arrived on campus. I was just a little ahead of my time.

Final Score: #9 Clemson 33 Georgia Tech 12

I always thought that it would be cool and couldn't wait to get passed up the stands. Advice to future mascots: stay away from your fraternity–Alpha Tau Omega, in my case–your sorority, or friends. Needless to say, it wasn't the experience I envisioned.

During a promotion at halftime of a soccer match, a child was selected to attempt a penalty kick against her hero, The Tiger. This was the easiest thing you have to do, especially when you have no peripheral vision. In my attempt to let the child win with a fake block, I accidentally blocked her kick. After realizing what I did, I kicked the ball in the goal. The jeers from the stands turned into cheers as the child won her prize.

At another soccer match, one of the ears on the headgear became loose. Like any athlete on the field, a trainer came to the rescue and took me to the locker room for repairs. When I reappeared in the stands with medical tape on the ear, a little girl noticed it and asked me if I  had a "boo boo." I shook my head yes and rubbed it like it hurt. She gave me a big hug and told me she hoped I felt better. It made me smile the rest of the day.

Parades and festivals are extremely hot as you walk around waiting for the event to begin. Once at a summer event in Newberry, I almost passed out from heat exhaustion. When the parade began, they put me on a fire truck. I remember holding my head up so the air flow would come through the mouth to cool me off. I looked like a dog hanging his head out of a car window. Today the helmet has a hole on top with a mesh cover to allow the heat to exit.

The individuals who organize local events for their community are great citizens. What can I say about those who coordinate the Gaffney Peach Festival when they give you a huge basket of peaches? Thank you! I headed directly to my Great Aunt Elwyna Jones's house in Easley. A couple of days later, everyone was enjoying delicious peach cobbler, compliments of the residents of Gaffney.

One of the nicknames of Charleston is the Holy City. Growing up in North Carolina, I had never been to Charleston. I told my fraternity brother David Dodds I had an appearance in Chucktown, another nickname for Charleston. His girlfriend Beth Albrecht, now his wife, who happened to live in Charleston, invited us to dinner with her family. Wow, a home-cooked meal. Sounded like a good deal to me! However, if it sounds too good, you know there must be something wrong. There was! I had to put the suit on after dinner. The life of a mascot is never ending.

BRIAN HOLDEN
No. 2 Tiger Fall 1987
Bachelor of Science in Accounting '87
Chairman and CEO
AR Funding
Residence - Greenville, S.C.
Hometown - Simpsonville S.C.

The Tigers were 6-0 and ranked seventh in the country in mid-October in 1987. The defending ACC champions were climbing up the polls under the play of running back Terry Allen, linebacker Michael Dean Perry, kicker David Treadwell, quarterback Rodney Williams, and defensive back Donnell Woolford, to name a few of the players.

Football is played in two halves and on this day, it was definitely a game of halves. NC State won the first half and Clemson the second half.

Down 30-0 going into the third quarter, the halftime speech by Coach Ford was one of his finest. He said nothing. If you have ever played for Coach Ford, you knew that was unusual, just like the first half. As the Tigers mounted their second half comeback, I was instructed to run the newly purchased 10'x15' Tiger Paw flag around the field (approximately 400 yards) to motivate the crowd. It looks easy; however, it becomes very difficult when running into just a little wind. It seemed like every couple of laps we would score, which meant stop and do a set of pushups. Then, off I went doing another lap with the flag. I don't remember how many laps; however, I wish we would have scored one more time.

Final Score: NC State 30   #7 Clemson 28

DARIUS JONES

No. 2 Tiger 1994-96
Bachelor of Fine Arts '96
Digital Imaging Lab Manager
Clemson University
Residence - Pendleton, S.C.
Hometown - Calhoun Falls, S.C.

During Mike Bays' first year as The Tiger in 1994, I was his roommate, spotter and cameraman. After one of his early football games, he allowed me to wear the suit at a tailgate. Mike was grooming me to be his No. 2 mascot along with Wes Scruggs and Rob Lockard. Next, I began attending volleyball matches. However, the real test came the next year when we decided to switch out at a women's basketball game, just to see if anyone would notice. As I was preparing to walk out of the tunnel, the advisor noticed Mike standing next to me and asked: "Who is that?" He grabbed the mask and looked into the eyehole and walked off. You could say that was my tryout, as Mike never suited up for another women's basketball game.

As a No. 2 mascot, you can create good memories for yourself by playing the drums with the pep band or rappelling from the rafters in Littlejohn Coliseum for the Tiger Paw Classic Gymnastics Invitational. Bays always hated when I did things like that, especially tumbling at the gymnastics meet, because people would expect him to do crazy stunts. However, he was scared of heights and lacked the gymnastic skills that I possessed.

In 1996, I was on the football field for Senior Day because Mike wanted his picture taken with The Tiger, so I got to work one quarter. Instead of it being the second of a six-game winning streak against the Cocks, it was the second win in three games for South Carolina.

Final Score: South Carolina 34 #22 Clemson 31

CORY LUCKETT
No. 2 Tiger 2006-08
Bachelor of Science in Management '08
Senior Product Manager
CoreLogic
Residence - Urbana, Md.
Hometown - Germantown, Md.

Not being selected to be The Tiger is a terrible feeling. However it did give me a chance to see and experience the mascot in a different way. My first year as the backup Tiger was fall of 2006, my junior year. After being backup throughout the year, I had the opportunity to try out again for the mascot position for my senior year. That next year, I had to make a video for my tryout since I was studying abroad in Italy during the in-person tryouts. My skit was catching a touchdown pass, followed by a celebration dance. I think the judges not physically being able to see me do my pushups or in the suit to do my dance were the main reasons why I was not selected as the No. 1 Tiger. However, college teaches you the ups and downs of life. How you adapt determines how successful you will be after college.

Putting the suit on for the first time was amazing. It feels like you are wearing history, which you are to some degree. As the No. 2 mascot, you get to rotate quarters with the No. 1 mascot. Therefore we both had two quarters of a football game to wear the suit. The worst time to be in the suit is in September, during a noon game, when it feels like it is 100+ degrees outside. The best is in November when it gets chilly outside. You can get in a warm suit while everyone else is freezing. However, when you take it off, and the cold air hits your sweaty body, it is like being thrown into a freezer!

The mascots are the face of the university without actually showing a face. You have the opportunity to make everyone a fan, especially the youngsters who might be leaning towards that "other" school in the state because their mom, dad, brother, sister, or grandparents did not attend Clemson. Youngsters between 8 and 12 years old begin to develop their own loyalties. Hopefully, because of our antics and fun personality, they will become Clemson fans.

WILLIAM "WILL" H. McCAULEY, III

No. 2 Tiger 1991-92
Bachelor of Science in
*   Construction Science and Management '93*
Commercial Contractor
Creative Builders, Inc.
Residence and Hometown - Greenville, S.C.

During the summer of 1991, I was living in the home vacated by former Coach Danny Ford. My roommate Will Sykes, the No. 1 Tiger who I always had to finish push-ups for, decided to travel out west for a couple of months. Our advisor called me up in his usual fashion, straight to the point with little detail: "Will, pick up the suit from the cleaners, you are headed to Hampton on Saturday." "OK, what for, boss?" He said, "The Hampton County Watermelon Festival Parade."

What? For those who have never heard of Hampton, drive east from Clemson to Columbia. Then, go south on I-26 until you get to the Orangeburg exit. Turn right onto US-601 and thirty minutes later you arrive in Hampton. This three and a half hour drive took me an extra hour. Mapquest was not around in the nineties.

Upon arrival, I got a quick history lesson on this nine-day festival. It features everything from a Watermelon Queen Pageant to the distinction of hosting the longest parade in the state at 3.2 miles.

Once in the suit, I was instructed by the parade organizers to run alongside the local high school cheerleaders' float and interact with the crowd. The "mascot code" was in effect: Don't speak or take off the head when in character no matter how hot you get.

A mile into the parade, I was gracefully clinging to the side of the float in desperation for water on this extremely hot June day. At the 1.5-mile marker, I threw myself onto the float yelling for water. A mile further, I was totally spread eagled on the float on my back with every cheerleader lined up taking turns dousing water through the eyes of the head. At the three-mile mark, I ripped the head off. Total panic had erupted on the float. Code or no code, it was time to save myself.

It was early evening when my arms and legs finally retracted back from a rubber band-drawn fetal position. I just need to give a shout out of thanks to all those cheerleaders who came to my rescue. After being assisted to my car, I successfully made the long drive back to Clemson.

It was mentioned in Will Sykes's section that the summer house we were living in had a pool. What a great sight to see all the female cheerleaders sunbathing. Will and I felt like we were in heaven. On the other hand, waking up at 8 a.m. to the sounds of the grounds crew mowing the yard was not exactly paradise for a couple of college boys. But then again, the Athletic Department had hired a pool cleaning company. When asked, "What did you do during the summer?" Sorry, the mascot code is in effect. Some things you cannot talk about.

Looking back, my proudest moment came in 1992 when I had the privilege to appear as The Tiger at the Greenville Chamber of Commerce's annual gala. My father, William (Billy) H. McCauley II was honored as the Business Entrepreneur of the Year. Lou Holtz was the keynote speaker.

My biggest regret was not taking advantage of exploiting the picture of me in the suit beside Lou holding up No. 1 sign years later when he was head coach for the chickens. Would have made a great billboard.

So there it is, from worst (parade) to best (house), from proudest (father) to regrettable (billboard). May the Paw reign forever!

BRIAN McGARRY
No. 2 Tiger 2008-10
Bachelor of Arts, Production Studies in
*   Performing Arts '09*
Financial Director
Chick-fil-A
Residence - Greer, S.C.
Hometown - Greenville, S.C.

My first experience in the suit was a brunch before the second home game of the 2008 football season against NC State. Upon arriving at the event, I was told to mingle with the guests but be near the host of the party. When

10:30 a.m. arrived, I was standing next to the host who gave a welcoming speech. He then brought his girlfriend up beside him and proposed. She, of course was ecstatic! To quote the host: "I am not a man for waiting, so is there a minister here?" Sure enough there was and the happy couple was married on the spot. The Tiger was the best man, and I even signed the marriage license as The Tiger.

Final Score: #23 Clemson 27 NC State 9

The next week I was back on the field firing the cannon for the South Carolina State University game. On cue during Tiger Band's pre-game performance, I fired the cannon, took off down The Hill, turned around, and...no football team. The previous time this had happened was in 2002, on the 100th anniversary of the Clemson-South Carolina series. There were so many fans outside the stadium, the buses could not get around to The Hill.

Final Score: #23 Clemson 54 SCSU 0

During the summer of 2009, I was at the ACC meetings in Greensboro, N.C. with all the other conference mascots and head football coaches. The mascots were in attendance to make a video that featured each head coach in a locker room trying to energize their team. In our case, it was only Coach Swinney in the video that was to be shown in Death Valley. Dabo's lines were simple, "We need to get out there, show support for the players, coaches and refs...etc." The camera then panned to the mascots and we all had blank stares. Coach then followed up with "Well, what do you say?" To which, we all jumped up and got excited. During the filming, I discovered that the Miami mascot, Sebastian the Ibis, has a hole in his mouth so he doesn't have to take the head off to get a drink. It sure would be nice to have that luxury with our Tiger costume.

By the end of the 2009 season, everyone was at the Music City Bowl in Nashville, Tenn. where I was fortunate enough to be in the suit at the end of the game for the trophy presentation. Magical moments in anyone's life can happen when you least expect it. For me it was walking off the field alongside C.J. Spiller with my family watching from the stands.

Final Score: Clemson 21 Kentucky 13

Each May, the Women's Alumni Council hosts a Bring Your Daughter to Clemson Weekend. On Sunday, in Memorial Stadium after C.J. Spiller was drafted by the Buffalo Bills in 2010, Heather Byrd ('99) from Goose Creek, brought a couple of Spiller jerseys we could wear for a picture at Howard's Rock.

A couple of weeks later, I was at a family gathering when my brother Mike started talking about a work associate he knew and described a picture she had posted on Facebook. Although it is our job to make moments special for the fans, on this occasion it was a special moment for me to tell my brother that I just happened to be The Tiger there in the Spiller jersey.

BRIAN PARK
No. 2 Tiger 2009-11
Bachelor of Science in Economics and
*   Political Science '10*
Master of Arts in Economics '14
Juris Doctor '14
University of Virginia
Attorney
King & Spalding LLP
Residence - Atlanta, Ga.
Hometown - Fort Mill, S.C.

Being in the right place at the right time is how many of us became the No. 2 Tiger or Cub. You either volunteer or someone volunteers you to help out at an event, especially if you are a student worker for the athletic department or alumni association.

As a member of Central Spirit, I had waved and carried one of the flags that spell C-L-E-M-S-(Tiger Paw)-N at a football game. My first time in the suit was at a basketball game in 2010. I exited the tunnel raising one of those football flags. As I pulled the flag pole to a vertical position, unbeknownst to me, I accidently hit two cheerleaders due to my lack of spatial awareness. Sorry, ladies, and here is my official apology.

The best prop we have as a mascot is our tail. Kids love to pull on it and we love to twirl it in a circle. Another use of the tail is as a guitar or if you are at an alumni event, a microphone. It would be an excellent recorder for all the story-telling about the good old days.

I was The Tiger at an alumni event in Washington one year, I believe in connection with the "Will to Lead Campaign." There were quite a few distinguished alumni in attendance. I was walking around and taking pictures with different groups and families. One alumna, who must have been at least 70 years old, wanted to send me, The Tiger, on my way with a little parting gift in the form of a vigorous squeeze to my backside. Completely surprised, I quickly spun around and returned a semi-flirtatious wave back at her, which was met with a wink. Apparently, The Tiger has timeless sex appeal.

CALEB REYNOLDS
No. 2 Tiger 2011-14
Bachelor of Science in Biological Sciences '14
Retired Mascot
Residence - Clemson, S.C.
Hometown - Lexington, S.C.

Most Tiger mascots are six feet or taller, whereas their counterpart, the Tiger Cub, is under six feet. I had an appearance at an elementary school in Pelzer when I discovered that I accidentally brought a Tiger Cub suit instead of a Tiger suit. At 6'2" everyone was able to see my ankles sticking out of the uniform for the next three hours. In addition, the suit was tight in certain areas. Use your imagination!

Moms, before you schedule an appearance of one of the mascots, make sure you know which one your child is in love with. Usually if your child is under four, schedule the Tiger Cub instead of The Tiger. How do I know this? At a birthday party in Easley, everyone there loved The Tiger except for the birthday girl, who sat in the corner crying until her mom asked me if I could leave early. I hope she had a great birthday after my departure.

Having been through the tryout phase a couple of times, I knew push-ups were important. You only have to do 50; however, I almost doubled that total by doing 93 as The Tiger on my final attempt to be the No. 1 mascot.

All the other mascots knew I was good in doing pushups, so when the score got over 50, I jumped into action. During the fourth quarter against South Carolina State in 2014, I did a total of 205 pushups while in The Tiger suit, giving me the new record for the number of pushups in the fourth quarter.

Final Score: #23 Clemson 73   SCSU 7

TEE SUBER
No. 2 Tiger 2001-04
Bachelor of Science in Recreation and
*   Park Administration '02*
Master of Human Resource Development '04
Assistant General Manager
Evolution Villages - Clemson West
Residence - Central, S.C.
Hometown - Whitmire, S.C.

The baseball stadium was called Beautiful Tiger Field when I was in college. Birthday parties were the norm on the Jervey Athletic Center balcony overlooking the baseball diamond. My first time in The Tiger suit was unexpected. One of the mothers of a party was upset that The Tiger was not going to be present for the game due to the end of the semester.

Working in game management, I was told to get into the suit. I didn't think about it too much, but I was nervous that I had to go into the baseball crowd to find the child and mom. My nervousness came from not wanting to mess up a tradition that I had admired since my childhood. As a college student, I had absolutely no desire to try out to be The Tiger out of fear I would not be able to replicate the motions or antics. It was a little nerve wracking. However, seeing the look on all those little faces was priceless!

In my apartment one night, I entered a sleeping roommate's room in full suit. I had on a Clemson baseball shirt and a bat in my hand. When I turned on the light, he quickly woke up. In my deepest and scariest voice, I told him Baseball Coach Jack Leggett sent me to invite him to Tiger Field to watch the Tigers play. When I left the room, I turned off the light and slammed the door. My roommate didn't mention anything for a while because he thought the whole thing was a dream. We told him the whole story a couple of weeks later.

Once again, while working in game management you have no idea what you might do on any given day. During the month of January, I would fire the cannon during football recruiting weekends when prospects toured Memorial Stadium. I remember Duane Coleman's visit because it was on a Monday, and he was on his way home to Miami from a trip to The Ohio State University.

In the fall, after Duane had signed with Clemson and was on campus, I caught up with him, and we talked about his recruiting trips. He thought it was pretty cool that we busted out the cannon for his visit. It doesn't matter who you are, you have to treat every official visit by a potential student-athlete the same whether they are by themselves or with a large group.

Lucas Glover, the newly crowned 2009 U.S. Open golf champion, was at Fluor Field in his hometown of Greenville. The community came together to celebrate his historic victory and I was lucky enough to be in The Tiger suit. As Andy Solomon, an athletic administrator at The Citadel would say, "It's a great day to be me." My dad Tommy played golf for the Tigers from 1967-71, and was the Medalist (Most Valuable Golfer) for the team in 1970.

You never know where you will change into the suit when at an appearance. My changing place for Bryn Gibson's wedding reception in Gaffney was in the pool house of the local sheriff's home. The sheriff was a personal friend of the bride and a big Gamecock fan. At the wedding, I randomly sat next to the sheriff's wife. Before she had a chance to figure out who I was, she looked over to me and stated, "I heard the Clemson Tiger was supposed to be here." I told her that would be neat. It was!

Jeanne Schmidt, the director of Camp Kemo in Batesburg for over 25 years, invited me, as The Tiger, Cocky, and members of the University of South Carolina basketball team to attend their annual camp pool party. Being surrounded by so many Gamecocks, I made sure to stay far away from the edge of the pool. Mrs. Schmidt enjoyed my appearance so much that she asked me to appear at her daughter's wedding several months later. Her daughter married a South Carolina rugby player. I was about to get assaulted by the rugby team when a high school teammate of mine realized that I was The Tiger and instructed the rugby players to stand off. The Schmidt family has helped so many people and has been an inspiration to many in their community. Upon hearing of Mrs. Schmidt's unexpected passing, I remember this night even more fondly.

DOW WELSH
No. 2 Tiger
Bachelor of Science in Parks, Recreation
and Tourism Management '94
Pastor
Holland Avenue Baptist Church
Residence - Lexington, S.C.
Hometown - North Augusta, S.C.

I'm probably the only Tiger not to have completed any pushups during a football game. Why? I was the mic man and The Tiger for several of the Olympic sporting events. I'm confident I could have done at least three pushups back then. Twenty years later, three pushups are still within reach.

One of my best moments in the suit was at a wrestling match watching two-time 118-pound national champion Sam Henson. Mascots and wrestlers have one thing in common. We both are used to dropping weight. Wrestlers drop weight prior to a match, whereas mascots can sometimes drop 10 pounds working an event.

Being The Tiger in the official parade in downtown Spartanburg celebrating the announcement of the NFL franchise for the Carolina Panthers was a great experience. It's high on my list just like being able to fly on the university plane with Coach Tommy West to an IPTAY meeting in Aiken with my parents and hometown friends in attendance. Another first-time experience for me was being at the groundbreaking ceremony for the Walker Course with Steve Melnyk, the course designer, in attendance. I recommend you play a round of golf or at least walk out to the 17th tee box to see the green and bunkers, together they form a Tiger paw.

In 1940 Winston Churchill was the prime minister of the United Kingdom. The story is told that he was decorating a shy young battle hero. Churchill allegedly said to him, "You feel very humble in my presence, don't you?" The young soldier replied, "Yes sir." Churchill replied, "Then perhaps you can imagine how humble and awkward I feel in yours." There is a similar feeling in fans from age 8 to age 80 when The Tiger walks up. Eyes get wide and smiles spread. The humble reality, though, is that inside the suit the eyes are just as wide and the smiles are just as big. Humbled, honored and full of joy. That sums up what it means to be The Tiger.

GLEN WILLIAMS
No. 2 Tiger 1990-91
Bachelor of Science in Management '91
Regional Director of Operations
Greenville Courtyard Marriott
Residence - Greer, S.C.
Hometown - Montvale, N.J.

The Tigers were 8-2 going into the 1990 game against South Carolina. Will Sykes was in The Tiger suit when I started a fire on a small grill in the end zone so we could cook chicken wings. The flames were flying high when they appeared on a television in the Memorial Stadium security box. The fire chief saw the flames and radioed an officer to tell us to extinguish the fire. Seems he was worried the suit would catch fire. It was something we never thought of, otherwise we would have tested the suit to see if it was flame retardant. Thank goodness we had a bucket of Kentucky Fried Chicken that we had purchased earlier that morning.

Final Score: #17 Clemson 24   South Carolina 15

As the No. 2 mascot, you never know when you will get the call from the bullpen, just like a relief pitcher. I got the call one afternoon and headed to the Oconee County Regional Airport to get on the university plane with Head Football Coach Ken Hatfield, along with several other coaches and administrators. We were flying to an IPTAY meeting at the Gator Bowl in Jacksonville, Fla. At the end of the evening after shaking hands and getting pictures taken with the fans, they fed me and gave me a check (a nice bonus). It was a pretty cool experience for any college student to fly on the university plane.

CHAPTER TEN
NO. 2 TIGER CUBS

ANDREW ROSS

No. 2 Tiger and No. 2 Tiger Cub 2007-08
Bachelor of Arts in Psychology '08
Police Officer 1
Residence and Hometown - Woodstock, Ga.

In basketball when you are too short to be a center or too tall to be a point guard, you play the forward position. In my case, at 5'11", I became the backup for both mascots because I could wear both suits.

During my tryout I did 45 pushups and stood up to hear the judges ask: "What if the Tigers scored more than 45 points?" I immediately dropped down and did 10 more. Looking back, I was still short of the 63 pushups Brad Stoehr did against South Carolina in that historic win in 2003 over the Gamecocks.

I grew up going to Clemson football games with my grandfather. The first time I was able to put on the Tiger Cub suit and make my way onto the field brought back nothing but memories of when I was young. However, the first time I was able to run down The Hill as the Tiger Cub was something special. I remember walking out of the tunnel, onto the field and straight towards The Rock on top of The Hill. I put both hands down on The Rock, looked to where my grandfather used to sit in the south stands

thinking to myself, this was for him. He taught me to bleed orange, and he taught me to always cheer for our Tigers with every ounce of energy I had. Running down The Hill at the sound of the cannon with the football team on my heels is something I know made him proud and why being a mascot was more than putting on a suit. Being a mascot is part of being the heart and soul of a family that bleeds orange.

In 2007, S.C. ETV was running a fund-raising event the Friday before the South Carolina game showing a documentary about Big Thursday. This was the annual football game between Clemson and South Carolina during the State Fair in Columbia. During commercials, Cocky and I entertained the television audience while the studio hosts asked for donations. Growing up a Clemson fan, it was an honor to help relive a tradition that ended in 1959.

"Are You OK with O.P.P." was at its peak when the Tar Heels came to play the 12-1 Tigers during Head Basketball Coach Oliver Purnell's fifth season in 2008.

It's a scary feeling when you black out in the suit. It happened to me after the Carolina game as I was going to the dressing room in Littlejohn Coliseum. Someone turned out the lights on me and the Tigers. The party was definitely over after the overtime loss.

Final Score: #1 North Carolina 90   #19 Clemson 88   OT

IAN McKENZIE
No. 2 Tiger Cub 2009-11
EMS and Disaster Relief School
UNC Wilmington
Confined Space Rescue and Safe Work Supervisor
JB Moore, LLC
Residence - Wilmington, N.C.
Hometown - Greenville, S.C.

Baseball games are usually the first appearance anyone makes as a mascot due to tryouts being held during baseball season. I forgot one of the two "Golden Rules." The first person I passed said, "How's it going Cub?" I answered, "Doing pretty good today, how about you? Wait, I can't talk. ROAR bye!"

The first football game that I ran down The Hill I was so pumped up that I didn't stop moving during the first quarter. When I finally took a break, I was sitting on the bench when Jacoby Ford sat next to me. One of the unexpected rewards for your hard work in the suit is sitting next to your favorite player. I wasn't in the same shape as Ford as I had to be administered two I.V.s of saline during the game.

During another football game I was in the stands when a female student latched onto me for a picture. She was crushing the life out of me. After the picture, she wouldn't let me go, and proceeded to yell, "Cub, be my boyfriend, let's get married!" When I pulled away, she lifted me off the ground and pinned me down to the bleacher. Despite my protest, everyone in the area laughed.

I remember walking out to the front gate of the soccer stadium in my suit waiting on The Tiger to arrive. He was running late, out of uniform, and it was almost time for the national anthem. As he began to cross the road from the parking lot he did not stop to look both ways and rolled onto the hood of a passing truck. I ran as fast as I could to see if he was okay. The nearby crowd stopped and began laughing thinking it was a skit. I helped my partner to his feet. He quickly changed into his suit and we barely made it to the sideline to stand next to the team during the anthem. Lesson to everyone, look both ways before crossing the road.

An incident happened while I was attending a wedding reception at the Shem Creek Bar and Grill in Mt. Pleasant. A sky lantern tribute to the newlyweds did not go as planned. I was set up nearby the launch area taking pictures under a flower archway. As I turned in the direction of screams, I saw a sky lantern flying straight towards me. A balloon section close by was already on fire. If I was out of the suit I would have assisted in the situation. In a furry costume, I decided to gracefully run in the other direction. No one got hurt and the fire was put out quickly. The bride and groom have a unique story to tell their children one day.

While working at an event for the Mauldin Miracle League for special needs children, there was one girl who was terrified of all mascots in attendance. Her parents came over to all of us and asked if we would give her space. Throughout the day, I noticed that this girl was watching me while her friends were getting pictures with the other mascots. When an announcement was made that the mascots would be leaving, the little girl asked her parents to find me. They came and said, "I can't believe it, but Susan wants to meet you. Please be aware that it might be too much for her, but if you're willing, we would like to introduce you." I followed them over to Susan and stopped about 10 feet away to let her come to me, and she did. I got a hug and a smile that will stay with me forever. Her parents were crying and I have never felt any better about being a mascot. The ultimate reward. Thank you, Susan!

MARSHALL SAUNDERS
No. 2 Tiger Cub 2010-12
Bachelor of Science in Agricultural
*   Mechanization and Business '12*
Quality Control Manager
Crown Orchard Company
Residence - Charlottesville, Va.
Hometown - Piney River, Va.

Having grown up 40 miles from Blacksburg, Va., many of my relatives—26, to be exact—had graduated or were enrolled at Virginia Tech. My grandfather, Paul Saunders, was serving as the president of the Virginia Tech Alumni Association in 2011. Our family picture was on the front page of the *Virginia Tech Magazine* that year minus this Cub, who just happened to go south to attend Clemson.

It was a bizarre feeling on this late October afternoon as the Clemson bus I was on rolled towards Lane Stadium having been a member of a diehard Hokie family since birth. The Hokie fan base is just as loyal to their athletic teams as the Clemson fans. There was Hokie orange and maroon throughout all the parking lots. Just as I remember when I was a youngster.

Upon exiting the bus, The Tiger and I were escorted to our dressing room to change into our suits. I could feel the air full of excitement as the two Top 20 teams prepared for battle.

The Hokie football team took the field first to the song, "Enter Sandman," as I was looking across to my parents' front row seats on the 12-yard line. Next to them, I eye-balled my old seat thinking that today, I'm a Tiger and not a Hokie. A few seconds later I had so much pride as I high-fived MY team as we charged the field.

Prior to the game I wondered did I make the correct decision to leave the state. I didn't take long to realize that yes, being a Tiger or in this case, the Cub, was my calling. The Tigers were leading 10-3 at halftime. By the end of the game, the Tigers won their third consecutive game over a ranked opponent, and ended the Hokies' 12-game winning streak. Until now, I didn't realize the significance the numbers 1 and 2 would play on my historic return to Lane Stadium. Together they are 12 (my old row and Virginia Tech's winning streak prior to the game). Separated by a line, they are ½ (my jersey number).

After the game, I remember a Hokie fan throwing a turkey leg bone towards me while I was being filmed by an ESPN cameraman. I quickly retrieved it and began using it as a prop as I chewed on it in front of the camera. Pretty sure the Hokie fan regretted tossing that leg. Afterwards the Hokie Bird and I had a duel followed by a big hug and a few goofy pictures.

Final Score: #13 Clemson 23   #11 Virginia Tech 3

Senior Day/Night is a special event and for the second year in a row the Tiger basketball team finished the regular season in 2012 against Virginia Tech. Tech was making a comeback during the second half when Jerai Grant stole the ball and made a slam dunk! I ran out on the court doing the cadence count thinking Tech would call a time out. As I turned around, the next thing I knew the ball was in play but the referee did not see me. Man, did I get an earful from game management. I was so embarrassed in front of my family. However the final score gave me bragging rights again over my Hokie relatives.

Final Score: Clemson 58   Virginia Tech 56

The 2010-11 men's basketball post-season began with a trip to Dayton, Ohio for a First Four game of the NCAA Tournament. The Tuesday night game saw the Tigers defeat the University of Alabama-Birmingham (70-52). The next day (Wednesday) we jet set to Tampa, Fla. for a second-round encounter against the University of West Virginia. Although the Tigers had a nine-point lead late in the first half, they ended up losing on Thursday evening (84-76) to the 22nd ranked Mountaineers.

Our flight back to Clemson was not leaving until Friday morning so several cheerleaders and myself decided to go see the Tampa nightlife. Waiting outside our hotel for a taxi, something caught the eye of this Tiger. It took me a brief moment to realize that it was "The Nature Boy," Ric Flair. I instantly wanted to go WOOOOO! I was too nervous to talk to him, as he is a 16-time World Heavyweight Wrestling Champion! I mean, this guy could pull the knife edge chop on me before I could say hello. So I wised up and told Kimberly Henderson, one of the cheerleaders, to go over to Flair and initiate conversation so we can get a picture. With her natural swagger, ability to talk to people, and beautiful Southern smile, it was no problem convincing Flair to get a picture with us.

After Flair graciously provided us with this photo opportunity, we started talking to his chauffeur. Flair was in Tampa to do a commercial for a chiropractic business. During our conversation, we mentioned we wanted to go out to a nice club for St. Patrick's Day. He paused for a minute and said he knew the perfect place and he'd give us a ride.

Wow! The story was getting better all the time as we piled in his black, all-leather interior BMW. Upon arrival, he told us he knew the owner and would get us in VIP. Sure enough we hopped out and walked right into the club to the roped off VIP section ahead of the 100+ people standing outside in line. After dancing the night away, we left the club feeling like the one and only Ric Flair, the Stylin', Profilin', Limousine Riding, Jet Flying, Kiss-Stealing, Wheelin' and Dealin' Son of a Gun!" WOOOOO!

CHAPTER ELEVEN
THE PRESIDENTIAL TIGER

JIM BARKER
The Presidential Tiger
Bachelor of Architecture '70
Dean/College of Architecture 1986-1995
Dean/College of Architecture, Arts
  and Humanities 1995-1999
Professor of Architecture 1986-present
Clemson University President 1999-2013
Clemson University President Emeritus
  2013-present
Residence - Clemson, S.C.
Hometown - Kingsport, Tenn.

To me, The Tiger has always been the symbol of the spirit and energy of Clemson University. Two of my Delta Kappa Alpha fraternity brothers were The Tiger while I was a Clemson student (Bob Harris '67 and Sam Coker '69). In my second year as university president and after being encouraged by several current students, I expressed my desire to be the mascot at a football game. Having admired those who had been The Tiger, I was nervous but very excited about the opportunity to be a part of such a wonderful tradition, and sometimes a university president just needs to have fun.

Our football team opened the 2001 season with a 21-13 win over Central Florida. As I watched the game, I knew that in just seven days I would be in front of all the Clemson and Wofford fans.

September 8, 2001: In my business suit, I was hosting over 200 guests in the President's Box. Just before halftime I excused myself after explaining to our guests that I would replace Patrick Hitpas as The Tiger at the start of the third quarter.

The Tiger Den, where the mascots change, is underneath the west end zone stands. There is no air conditioning, hardly any light and a low-angle ceiling. It's a tight area with no shower, bathroom, or water faucets – just a curtain to hide the mascots from the photographers who work in front of this area. One of the mascots replaced the metal chairs with a sofa and a television (with no power) that doesn't have power to provide some comfort for the mascots when they take a break and have a box lunch.

When I got to the west end zone, I was directed to the officials' locker room to change into a clean Tiger suit. This was a good sign as I would need a quick shower after my appearance to get back to the President's Box. Our game management personnel do an outstanding job of anticipating the needs of our fans and, in this case, my need to get back to our guests.

My entrance to the field was the same as the football Tigers. As I began the journey out in front of the 79,158 fans, I could feel the sweat rolling down my forehead. I had only had the suit on for a couple of minutes! I thought, I sure could use a headband. The adrenalin built as I crossed the 50-yard line behind the Clemson bench and headed toward the student section.

It's not too often that The Tiger gets a police escort, but this time Patrolman Rick Clark ('00) of the Clemson Police Department guided me to the east end zone. As I waved to the crowd, I wondered if anyone noticed that this Tiger was different from the one in the first half. First of all, I was smaller in size. Second, did anyone notice I was wearing a new pair of Nike shoes? The shoes give away who is in the suit. Upon reaching the ROTC cadets who hold up the pushup board, I realized I had no idea how to get on or off. We hadn't rehearsed anything – just like all the other Tigers, everything would be impromptu for this rookie.

All first-time mascots have to learn how to see and to breathe. My overwhelming thought was, when will we score so I can do my pushups and get out of this hot suit?! I walked over to The Hill, hoping and praying that we would score on our first drive of the third quarter.

As I walked around and waited for the Tigers to score, I posed for photos with the students and others on the field. I was smiling for each photo … and I later laughed when I realized after 10 or so photos that no one could see me smile. Finally, after more than 30 minutes–it seemed like hours–the moment had arrived.

On this 500-degree September afternoon (OK, it felt like 500 degrees),

J.J. McKelvey successfully caught a seven-yard pass from Woody Dantzler and an Aaron Hunt extra point followed. The Tigers were up on Wofford 31-14. When "Tiger Rag" concluded, all eyes in Death Valley were aimed toward me in the southeast end zone for the traditional pushups. On this occasion, there would be a mere 31 pushups – a walk in the park for a veteran mascot. For this rookie, it would be like competing in an Ironman contest!

There I was, up on the board as I began my 31 pushups. I could hear the count with each pushup: 1, 2, 3, 4... 24, 25, 26, is this ever going to end, 27, 28, 29, 30, just an extra point to go and mission accomplished. Finally, number 31. Wow!!! It was an experience of a lifetime (and the ultimate bucket list event for any Clemson graduate). However, I'll leave it to a 19- to 21-year-old student.

It had to be one of the happiest moments of my life when I removed The Tiger head – I could breathe! Best of all, I could see the Clemson students' faces in complete surprise as they recognized who was in the suit!

The responses were remarkable and inspiring from students and alumni. Even now, once a week or so, someone fondly reminds me of my three appearances as The Tiger. During every commencement ceremony after my first appearance, when a graduating mascot crossed the stage and shook my hand as president, I felt an instant and special bond with the person wearing the Tiger "hands." It was a bond that I will always share with these ambassadors of our university.

I will always be grateful for this experience, but I would be remiss if I did not mention that after my third and final appearance in 2012, I received a letter from 26 of my fellow mascots asking me not to remove the head in the future. It was a very respectful letter, saying that the mascot should remain anonymous. I saw their point and responded that of course I would abide by their request. These students are a special component of who we are as a university. Their loyalty is unquestionable. The hours in the suit spent reaching out to everyone create an excitement and devotion to Clemson that cannot be measured. The Tiger and Tiger Cub are revered symbols, just as the Tiger Paw is, and we owe the people inside the suit a debt of gratitude.

PRESIDENTIAL FOOTBALL APPEARANCES

Sept. 8, 2001 – 31 Pushups
McKelvey 7-yard pass from Dantzler (Hunt kick) 3rd Quarter 0:10
(Actual time in the suit about 45 minutes)
Weather – 500 degrees according to this rookie mascot
Attendance: 79,158

Final Score: #20 Clemson 38   Wofford 14

Sept. 15, 2012 – 27 Pushups
Ellington 1-yard run (Catanzaro kick) 3rd Quarter, 12:10
(Actual time in the suit about 10 minutes)
Weather – Partly cloudy, 85 degrees
Attendance: 83,574

Final Score: #11 Clemson 41   Furman 7

PRESIDENTIAL BASKETBALL APPEARANCE

ESPN "College Gameday" – Jan. 23, 2010
Halftime score when introduced as The Tiger 23-23
(Actual time in the suit about 10 minutes)
Attendance: 10,000

Final Score: #7 Duke 60   #17 Clemson 47

CHAPTER TWELVE
ALL-TIME PUSHUP RECORDS

1st Quarter: 70 by Chris Alston   56-20 win vs. Duke (2012)

2nd Quarter: 175 by Ricky Capps   82-24 win vs. Wake Forest (1981)

3rd Quarter: 225 by "Kit" Southwick 59-38 win vs. North Carolina (2011)

4th Quarter: 205 by Caleb Reynolds 73-7 win vs. S.C. State (2014)

Single Game: 389 by Ricky Capps
76 by Wake Forest Demon Deacon Chris Kibler
82-24 win vs. Wake Forest (1981)

Home Day Game: 389 by Ricky Capps
76 by Wake Forest Demon Deacon Chris Kibler
82-24 win vs. Wake Forest (1981)

Home Night Game: 135 by Jon Potter
38-0 win vs. The Citadel (2000)

Away Day Game: 251 by Zack Mills
51-6 win vs. Wake Forest (1978)

Away Night Game: 315 by Brad Stoehr
63-17 win vs. South Carolina (2003)

Overseas Game: 72 by Randy Faile
21-17 win vs. Wake Forest in Tokyo (1982)

Bowl Game: 196 by Patrick Hitpas
49-24 win vs. La. Tech in Humanitarian Bowl (2001)

Season: 1,549 by Jon Potter (2000)

Career: 2,216 by Mike Bays (1994-97)

CHAPTER THIRTEEN
ESPN "COLLEGE GAMEDAY"

The biggest secret each week in college football is which headgear Lee Corso will choose on Saturday. It starts when Corso calls one of two sports information directors. Here at Clemson, it is Tim Bourret who answered the phone as Corso said, "I am picking Clemson this week. Can you arrange for me to get the headgear?" The week of Monday, October 16, 2006, the mascot advisor was the second and last person to know this classified secret. A call was placed to Mr. Corso and he said, "I need your Tiger head on Saturday, I'm picking Clemson over Georgia Tech." Then you swear not to tell anyone and you don't. The only way Corso changes his pick is if a key player gets injured at practice during the week leading up to the game. In our case it would have been "Thunder and Lighting" James Davis and C.J. Spiller, respectively.

Upon arrival to campus, Mr. Corso told a story to Bourret and the advisor about coaching at Indiana University. He said, "I told my players if we ever got the lead over Ohio State, I would stop the game and take a picture of the scoreboard. We scored a touchdown to take a 7-0 lead when I called a timeout, and told everyone to go to the middle of the field. Woody Hayes was going crazy on the other sideline." All Clemson fans know what that looks like. Hayes was yelling at the referee. He told Hayes that Corso called a timeout and could do whatever he wanted. Corso got his picture but Ohio State got the win. Now you know why Corso's personality makes "Gameday" so much fun to watch.

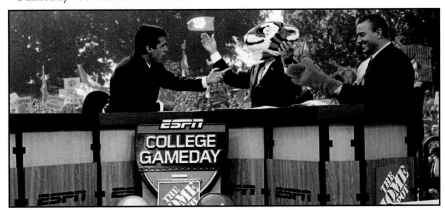

On Saturday, with the best Tiger head in a black trash bag, the mascot advisor went to Bowman Field and entered the ESPN bus. A couple of hours later, Corso put The Tiger head on to the delight of all the Clemson faithful!

2006 Final Score:	#12 Clemson 31	#13 Georgia Tech 7
2013 Final Score:	#8 Clemson 38	#5 Georgia 35
2013 Final Score:	#5 Florida State 51	#13 Clemson 14
2015 Final Score:	#11 Clemson 24	#6 Notre Dame 22

CHAPTER FOURTEEN
MASCOT MOMS

LAURA ALSTON, MOTHER OF TIGER CHRIS ALSTON

My first reaction was, "You have no cheerleading experience." Chris quickly told me that being The Tiger is not a cheerleading position. And he was so right! Being The Tiger requires creativity, organization, strength, discipline, and a large time commitment to your university.

After Chris became The Tiger, I became Tiger Mom 1 and Chris, Sr. became Tiger Dad 1. Chris and I talked a lot in his first year about weddings and what he might encounter. Looking back, I'm sure a lot of parents are glad we made him attend the Cotillion, where he learned how to dance.

We took Chris's 86-year-old grandmother to the game at University of Maryland so she could see him as The Tiger. It was an 8 p.m. game. We got her back home to her house around 2 a.m.!

Chris was hired at one of the university's job fairs before graduating. The CEO of the company, KeyMark, Inc., that hired him had been the mascot Duke Dog at James Madison University. I hope this cat and dog get along together for a long time.

TERESA BAYS, MOTHER OF TIGER MIKE BAYS

I remember Mike describing his first appearance at a Special Olympics event on campus assisting special needs children in a race. A young child grabbed his hand and helped him along by saying "I will help you finish the race, Tiger." Mike said he could not contain the tears he shed under his disguise. What parent wouldn't cry hearing a story like that?

When we picked Mike up from Clemson over Christmas break, he had the suit with him to do some appearances. One appearance was at a wrestling meet 90 miles away from our home in Bethlehem, Pa. at Bloomsburg, Pa. Needless to say, the Clemson wrestlers upon recognizing their mascot went on to thoroughly defeat Bucknell University 23-12 and James Madison University 19-13.

Lastly, my husband Gary, and I would like to comment on how well Mike was treated by the Clemson Family during his years as The Tiger. The kindness, hospitality, and generosity were a comfort to his parents who resided 700 miles away. Mike would tell us how well he was treated at away games and tournaments. We subsequently relocated to South Carolina in 1996 and were introduced to many of those wonderful people who were responsible for allowing our son to have a wonderful experience as The Tiger. Your friendships helped form our son into the fine young man he is today. We thank you for allowing us to express our fond memories as parents of The Tiger.

LISA HAMMETT, MOTHER OF TIGER ANDREW BEELER

During those first football games of the season, there was always the maternal fear of heatstroke! Ninety-degree temperatures, lots of pushups, and a hot Tiger suit are a bad combination. I was always thankful when late September/early October rolled around. I was also never a fan of The Tiger crowd-surfing to the top of the lower deck at Death Valley. I just closed my eyes as my husband Scotty kept reminding me, "He's gonna be OK."

The athletes he has met, the television personalities he has had his picture made with, the fellow Tigers and opposing mascots with whom he has formed friendships, the places he has traveled, the numerous Clemson

fans who have had their picture made with him, all pale in comparison to the joy that Andrew has received from doing something he loves for his university.

Knowing how much work goes on before and during football games, I once asked him during his senior year if he ever wished he could be one of those carefree students in the stands enjoying the tailgating and the game with no responsibilities. He said, "No, I don't wish that – those 81,000 people wish they were me."

JACKIE COLE, MOTHER OF TIGER NOLAN COLE

Upon putting the Tiger head on, my husband Rex thought it was cool and wondered how in the world they could do what they do without much vision. I, on the other hand, about gagged! I really don't know how Nolan tolerated the smell! Whew ... I just knew you had to be one tough person to wear that headgear.

At a pre-game pep rally, a mother holding her young daughter approached Nolan. Once she got his attention, the mother asked her daughter, "OK, do you remember what you promised?" As she got done saying that, the daughter slowly took the Binky from her mouth and handed it to The Tiger and then continued to look at him with a star-struck look. Nolan took the Binky with him and still has it on his trophy case to this day.

Parents, you need to be prepared to feel an overwhelming sense of PRIDE when your son or daughter becomes a mascot, whether in college or high school. The games they appear at take on a whole new meaning!

GAIL LICATA, MOTHER OF TIGER DANIEL LICATA

Seeing my son on national television at the 2007 Chick-fil-A Bowl in Atlanta was pretty amazing. We were celebrating New Year's Eve at our friend's home, and they had the game on their television. It was great for our friends to see Daniel as the Clemson Tiger in full-mascot mode.

Dan graduated summa cum laude from Clemson in 2009. We attended his graduation and were so proud, excited, and thrilled to see him approach the president of the university to receive his diploma. As his name was called, the crowd started to get excited, and we looked down to see Dan walk up to the president to shake his hand and accept his diploma, while wearing the Tiger Paws!! We were so happy to see him with a HUGE grin on his face (the local paper printed this embrace in their paper the next day) and waving to the crowd. The president also had a BIG smile on his face as he shook Dan's paw.

PAULA McGARRY, MOTHER OF TIGER BRIAN McGARRY

A great night for any fan is when you are in attendance at a game when there is a special announcement. For our family, it was when C.J. Spiller announced at a basketball game that he was coming back for his senior year. Brian was The Tiger on the floor, along with C.J., Coach Swinney, and the Tiger Cub.

MARGIE NICHOLS, MOTHER OF TIGER CHASE NICHOLS

Who wouldn't want to be The Tiger?! So of course we had to try on the suit. But since I'm much shorter than The Tiger, the crotch was almost dragging on the floor. Chase's sister, Morri, a 1992 Clemson graduate, also joined in the fun. We were trying to walk like The Tiger, with that bounce that Chase had in his step. I just remember laughing so hard, we cried!

There's nothing like watching people's reactions to The Tiger when he appears unexpectedly, like when we drove through downtown Clemson with him standing up out of our sunroof. He definitely turned heads and brought smiles ... as usual!

JANE POTTER, MOTHER OF TIGER JON POTTER

I knew it was a big commitment to be The Tiger and wondered if he would be able to keep up with his studies after two semesters of straight A's! After a month, my worries were over, as I spent more time watching The Tiger and the Tiger Cub than I did watching the game.

Moms, if your husband needs a workout, then meet up with your son or daughter after the game, and have him carry their suit back to the laundry room. It's the least he can do for them since you will probably be cooking a meal for everyone before the night is over.

LYNNE ROSS, MOTHER OF TIGER AND TIGER CUB ANDREW ROSS

Our son Andrew was both The Tiger and the Tiger Cub. We called him the "Chubby Cubby" because he filled up that suit! He was usually the Cub for the football games, so I was glad he didn't have to do all of those pushups.

The most memorable time we saw Andrew was at his first football game as the Tiger Cub. We went to Tiger Band's pre-game concert in the amphitheater. My daughter Carrie was a freshman that year at Clemson and my nephew Matthew Jones was in the band and his brother Robert was in Tigeroar, an all-male a cappella singing group on campus. As I sat there, watching, I was reminded of my daddy Amos and got very emotional. I think Andrew's desire to be the mascot was because of his "Pop." My dad loved Clemson. Even though he did not have the opportunity to attend college, he instilled in Andrew a great love for Clemson. I know he must have been smiling down from Heaven seeing his grandchildren so involved in Clemson University.

One day we were walking in downtown Clemson, looking in the shops. There was this giant picture of Andrew running down The Hill ahead of the team, with his arms up in the air like some kind of a super hero. Needless to say, two of those pictures were purchased, framed, and are hanging in our homes!

SUE SOUTHWICK, MOTHER OF TIGER CHRISTOPHER "KIT" SOUTHWICK

When Chris told us he was trying out, it just so happened that his high school soccer coach Jeff Moulton was Champ, the mascot for the Vermont Lake Monsters, a minor league baseball team. We called Jeff and asked for advice. It came in three parts. First, be big and slow, so you don't scare the kids and they have a chance to focus on your costume. Second, never try to out-macho a male fan. Finally, be "smoochy" with the girls. Advice well taken.

KATHY STOEHR, MOTHER OF TIGER BRAD STOEHR

Bradley's grandparents were able to travel from Florida to Atlanta for the 2004 Chick-fil-A Bowl. They told everyone they knew to watch the game and look for their grandson as The Tiger. Later, when everyone had gone out to celebrate the win, Bradley dressed up in the suit to surprise his grandparents with a personal appearance. That time with family and those pictures are priceless.

As a little boy, Bradley learned American Sign Language. I am an interpreter for the deaf, so I used sign language with Bradley and his sister. At an appearance at the South Carolina School for the Deaf and the Blind as The Tiger, Bradley communicated with the students and staff using ASL. The deaf children and adults do not expect guests from the outside community to be able to use sign language. They were so amazed to see that Bradley could understand them and talk to them in their language. Even though Bradley was working with some limitations – not enough digits to fingerspell effectively – he made such a connection that day. (For those who don't know, The Tiger has only four fingers.)

JANE SYKES, MOTHER OF TIGER WILL SYKES

Will's little sister Jane Wall suffered brain damage as a toddler and lost her ability to speak. One day, Will put the suit on and talked to her and she was so excited and expressive that we all knew she recognized his voice. He knew the rule, The Tiger could not talk when in the suit but Will broke it that one time for his sister. Will always enjoyed appearances at the hospitals and festivals where children of all ages were in attendance.

After Will had graduated, he was asked to fill in at a basketball game. We took his two sons at the time, five-year old Barber and three-year old

Craven, to see their dad. At halftime, we went onto the court and as Barber ran out to his dad, Craven said, "That might not be my dad." He wouldn't get close.

Mascots are treated like royalty anywhere they go. They are given keys to the city, ride in convertibles, are guests in homes, and spend time with town dignitaries and beauty queens. However, no matter where Will went he found the Clemson Spirit shining bright throughout the state of South Carolina and to this day he can shout above the crowds, GO TIGERS!!

Will would say, "What an honor and awesome experience it was to represent Clemson University as The Tiger!"

KELLY ADAMS, MOTHER OF TIGER CUB LAUREN ADAMS

In Lauren's section of this book, you read about Madelyn, a young girl in the hospital. It bears repeating what Lauren and other students do as mascots representing their university.

I would meet Lauren at events for safety depending upon where her appearance was on any given day. The one I am most proud of was after an event in Charleston. She stopped by Palmetto Richland Hospital in Columbia to meet Madelyn for the first time. We had received several phone calls and Facebook notifications that if Lauren was near her home of Irmo, Madelyn would love to see the Tiger Cub.

Wow, what a life-changing event! I stood back in awe with tears flowing. I could not imagine the impact it would leave on both Lauren and Madelyn's family. Upon seeing and playing with Madelyn, Lauren was asked if she minded going room to room to see others and bring a smile to their faces. It was all I could do as a parent to keep dry eyes!

A year later, it was almost Christmas. We called Madelyn's family and asked if they would like for the Tiger Cub to visit Madelyn, who was back in the hospital. Madelyn had not smiled in weeks, and they were just longing to see her smile one more time. When we arrived at the hospital, we saw how weak she was. Madelyn managed to have a little fun during the visit. A few weeks later, Madelyn passed away.

For our daughter, a 22-year-old, this will forever be in her heart. Clemson gave her an opportunity to be a part of something so special!

KAY ALEWINE, MOTHER OF TIGER CUB TYLER ALEWINE

As a parent, it was fun to watch people laugh at Tyler's antics. Until he became the Cub, I never realized just how many activities that the mascots participate in: games, parades, wedding receptions, rehearsal dinners, retirement parties, birthday parties, etc... There were times where he had two or three appearances in a day and, occasionally, we would help out by driving him so he could stay in character in order for him to make the next appearance on time.

Tyler and Cocky were at a formal wedding reception in Charleston one weekend. This was one of Tyler's first appearances so we took him to the venue. I could see only through a side door, but I was nervous about the two rival mascots. They worked really well together, as the bride and groom and their guests had a great time. Moms never stop worrying and always want to keep an eye on their child, even through a side door.

KAREN CAMPBELL, MOTHER OF TIGER CUB
SAMANTHA CAMPBELL

It's not too often our younger daughter Samantha can out-do her older sister Kristen in her own backyard of Charleston. They wore their respective mascot suits in downtown one day. Samantha was dressed as the Tiger Cub and Kristen as Clyde the Cougar. Those visiting the oldest city in South Carolina were attracted to the younger sister when they asked for a picture of the two mascots.

You are never too young to be a Tiger fan, especially if that person is your eight-year-old nephew Everett, attending Parents Weekend. We will find out in 10 years if Everett will follow Kristen's and Lauren's footsteps into a mascot suit. If he does, we hope he chooses one of these two universities and not that other school – South Carolina.

CAROLINE JERNIGAN, MOTHER OF TIGER CUB MARTIN DREW JERNIGAN

One thing my son, Martin Drew, failed to inform me about was that he intended to perform the dangerous stunt of sliding down the stair rail at a home basketball game. He knew that I would worry and try to talk him out of this performance since there was a high probability of getting hurt. But how could you ever question your child's motives when his presence at sporting events and community activities could only enhance the university's reputation? I remember how proud I was of Martin Drew when he made a Halloween visit as the Tiger Cub to a nursing home in our hometown, bringing joy to the patients, especially my mother and father.

BETH CRONIN, MOTHER OF TIGER CUB SARAH NEWBURN

Sarah's boyfriend Collin, now her husband, couldn't have been more proud of Sarah being the Tiger Cub, being that he is a sports enthusiast. She learned a lot about football as the Cub. Today, they drive from Chicago to attend Clemson games and, of course, visit with family, which is their second priority!

Sarah's dream was to have her rehearsal dinner in the west end zone of Memorial Stadium. That dream came true, along with their engagement pictures on the football field, like so many other Clemson couples.

MARIAN WILLIAMS, MOTHER OF TIGER CUB JAY WILLIAMS

I had always loved The Tiger and suggested to Jay that he try out. He replied, "You have to be six feet tall." I thought how nice it would be to have a baby tiger. Little did I know that one day I would get the call from Jay that he would be the first Tiger Cub mascot!

Like all the other moms, we too have a scrapbook of our son as a mascot.

P.S. – "Mom, we are not a baby Tiger, we are the nephew, going to college."

CHAPTER FIFTEEN
THE SUITS

The suits for The Tiger and Tiger Cub are made by Scollon Productions in White Rock just outside of Columbia on I-26.

After an order is placed, the mold for the head is retrieved from the storage warehouse and the pattern for the fur parts of the suit are located in the sewing room files.

The fur fabric is 80 percent acrylic and 20 percent polyester with a backing that's 75 percent polyester and 25 percent cotton. The head is fabricated via thermal-forming in Kydex plastic.

The surface of the head may require sanding, which is done, and then the appropriate helmet (usually a skate helmet) is installed into the costume head. All edges around the neckline are sanded and then a rough-edge trim is applied to the edge. The Tiger eyes are fabricated from acrylic spheres, cut in half, and then the back is painted with the eye detail. The head then moves into the sewing room where it is covered with the fur.

While the head is being prepared for covering in the shop, the sewing room is tracing the pattern onto the fur, cutting the body parts out, and then sewing them together to produce the body. The white belly and black striping details are cut separately and then stitched onto the orange suit.

The Tiger Cub shoes are a replica of a Nike shoe worn by the athletic teams.

Scollon Productions have produced mascot suits for over 200 colleges and universities, including the Duke Blue Devil, North Carolina Rameses, Pittsburgh Panther, and the Virginia Tech Hokie Bird.

"TALE OF THE TAPE"

	The Tiger	Cub
Neck	16"	15"
Sleeve	35"	34"
Height	6'1"	5'6"
Hips	42"	42"
Waist	36"	30"
Inseam	34"	34"
Helmet Size	Large	11 7/8"
Tail	56"	48"
Shoe Size	Varies	28

CHAPTER SIXTEEN
GAMEDAY SCHEDULE

Countdown To Kickoff	Event
4:00 Hr.	Tailgate with family
2:45	Arrive at the Tigers Den to change into the suit
2:15	Tiger Walk - Lot 5 - #1 Tiger and #1 Cub
1:30	Letterwinners Room - Littlejohn Coliseum - #2 Tiger or #2 Cub
1:00	Parade - #2 Tiger and #2 Cub
0:45 Min.	President's Box - #2 Tiger or #2 Cub
0:30	#1 Tiger and #1 Cub on the field
0:05	Kiss The Rock
0:03	Cannon fires. Run down The Hill
Kickoff	#1 Tiger and #1 Cub on the Field
2nd Quarter	#2 Tiger and #2 Cub on the Field
Halftime	Food, drink and an occasional IV in the Tiger Den #3 Tiger in the suites
3rd Quarter	#1 Tiger and #1 Cub - Crowd Surfing
4th Quarter	#2 Tiger and #2 Cub on the Field
0:00	Alma Mater at midfield
Postgame	Take the wet suit to be washed in the Jervey Athletic Center Laundry Room. Two hours later arrive back to the dorm-apartment after a little tailgating for a long cat nap.

CHAPTER SEVENTEEN
MASCOT MYSTICS

Many people wonder why The Tiger has worn different numbers since near the end of the 20th century. It started when the football coaches approached the administration about an incoming freshman Anthony Downs, who wanted to wear his same high school jersey number (No. 4) in college. The number, which had been worn by Clemson Hall of Fame quarterback Steve Fuller, was retired.

The request was approved at the same time the administration announced the formation of the Ring of Honor to recognize Clemson's greatest in all sports. To be a member of the Ring, you have to not only perform at the highest level on the field, but you had to complete your degree. To avoid any further conflicts, The Tiger switched from No. 1 to No. 00, and then to No. 0.

In 2012, the administration approached Head Football Coach Dabo Swinney about switching The Tiger's number back to No. 1. Coach Swinney said yes to the change, which is the goal of every Clemson team.

Why does the Tiger Cub wear the number No. ½ and big shoes? The administration wanted a mascot to appeal to the very young Clemson fans. Thus, the big shoes like Mickey Mouse, the friendlier face, and overalls. The No. ½ was chosen because the mascot was going to be shorter than The Tiger.

	NO. 1 TIGER	NO. 1 TIGER CUB
2015-16	Jonathan Mace	Deanne Flanders
2014-15	Andrew Beeler	Lauren Adams
2013-14	Chris Alston	Samantha Campbell
2012-13	Chris Alston	Kacie Trojanowsky
2011-12	Chris Alston	Sarah Newburn
	Chris Southwick	
2010-11	Michael Speer	Sarah Newburn
2009-10	Nolan Cole	Sarah Newburn
2008-09	Nolan Cole	Martin Drew Jernigan
2007-08	Dan Licata	Tyler Alewine
2006-07	Brandon Little	Clint Cagle
2005-06	Brandon Little	Clint Cagle
2004-05	Brad Stoehr	Paul Huguley
2003-04	Brad Stoehr	Paul Huguley
2002-03	Patrick Hitpas	Jordan Powell
2001-02	Patrick Hitpas	Kate Weppner

	NO. 1 TIGER	**NO. 1 TIGER CUB**
2000-01	Jon Potter	Dan Wangerin
1999-00	Zack Callaham	Dan Wangerin
1998-99	Rob Lockard	Dan Wangerin
1997-98	Wes Scruggs	Ryan Teten
1996-97	Mike Bays	Ryan Teten
1995-96	Mike Bays	Brian Gerhart
1994-95	Mike Bays	Jay Williams
1993-94	Chase Nichols	Jay Williams
1992-93	Chris Peters	
1991-92	Will Sykes	
1990-91	Will Sykes	
1989-90	Stuart McWhorter	
1988-89	Martin Lowry	
	Stuart McWhorter	
1987-88	Martin Lowry	
1986-87	Chris Shimakonis	
1985-86	David Friedman	
1984-85	Jay Watson	
1983-84	Randy Faile	
1982-83	Randy Faile	
1981-82	Ricky Capps	
1980-81	Ricky Capps	
1979-80	Zack Mills	
1978-79	Zack Mills	
1977-78	Randy Addison – football	
	Chris Carter - basketball	
1976-77	George Langstaff – football	
	David Baird – basketball	
1975-76	Tony Saad	
1974-75	Tony Saad	
1973-74	Mike Hunt	
1972-73	Mike Hunt	
1971-72	Randy Jackson	
1970-71	Randy Jackson	
1969-70	Sam Coker	
1968-69	Bob Dotson	
1967-68	Bob Harris	
1966-67	John "Zeke" Welborn	
1965-66	Marvin "Poag" Reid	
1963-64	Jim Gibson	
1961-62	Jim Lloyd	
1960-61	Steve Morrison	
1959-60	Billy McCown	
1957-58	Tommy Grant	
Early 1950s	Roy Southerlin	

CHAPTER EIGHTEEN
THE REUNION

The true authors of this book were the students who have worn The Tiger or Tiger Cub suit. As the Athletic Department mascot advisor, I stayed behind the scenes, organizing tryouts, appearances, and maintenance on the suits.

What is amazing to me about these students is that not one has ever mentioned how difficult it was to make a visit to a hospital. If you ever had to visit a sick family member or friend, you know what I am talking about.

There were plenty of times when I begged and pleaded with these outstanding students to do appearances when I knew they were tired, had a class, or an upcoming test. They were, and still are, pushed hard to make as many appearances as requested – over 300 a year, not counting home athletic events, and away football and post season basketball games.

I want to thank all the mascots for being great ambassadors for Clemson University, and for the stories that made this book possible. I know for some it was a trip down memory lane filled with laughter and tears of joy and sometimes sadness.

To all members of the Clemson Family, please accept my apology for times when a mascot was not in attendance at an event due to an overbooking or when I was unable to secure a mascot due to their personal schedule. I know how much The Tiger and the Tiger Cub mean to the Clemson Family. For 26 years, it was an honor to help coordinate the thousands of appearances. Thank you, to some of Clemson's finest. Semper Fi!

John Seketa
Honorary Clemson Alum '13